This book should be returned to any branch of the Lancashire County Library on or before the date shown

Lancashire County Library
Bowran Street
Preston PR1 2UX

Lancashire
County Council

www.lancashire.gov.uk/libraries

CHANDOS
INFORMATION PROFESSIONAL SERIES

Chandos' new series of books are aimed at the busy information professional. They have been specially commissioned to provide the reader with an authoritative view of current thinking. They are designed to provide easy-to-read and (most importantly) practical coverage of topics that are of interest to librarians and other information professionals. If you would like a full listing of current and forthcoming titles, please visit our web site **www.library-chandospublishing.com** or contact Hannah Grace-Williams on email info@chandospublishing.com or telephone number +44 (0) 1865 884447.

New authors: we are always pleased to receive ideas for new titles; if you would like to write a book for Chandos, please contact Dr Glyn Jones on email gjones@chandospublishing.com or telephone number +44 (0) 1865 884447.

Bulk orders: some organisations buy a number of copies of our books. If you are interested in doing this, we would be pleased to discuss a discount. Please contact Hannah Grace-Williams on email info@chandospublishing.com or telephone number +44 (0) 1865 884447.

The Digital Age and Local Studies

PETER H. REID

Chandos Publishing

Oxford · England · New Hampshire · USA

09414974

Chandos Publishing (Oxford) Limited
Chandos House
5 & 6 Steadys Lane
Stanton Harcourt
Oxford OX29 5RL
UK
Tel: +44 (0) 1865 884447 Fax: +44 (0) 1865 884448
Email: info@chandospublishing.com
www.library-chandospublishing.com

Chandos Publishing USA
3 Front Street, Suite 331
PO Box 338
Rollinsford, NH 03869
USA
Tel: 603 749 9171 Fax: 603 749 6155
Email: BizBks@aol.com

First published in Great Britain in 2003

ISBN:
1 84334 051 8 (paperback)
1 84334 052 6 (hardback)

© Peter H. Reid, 2003

British Library Cataloguing-in-Publication Data.
A catalogue record for this book is available from the British Library.

Typeset by Monolith – www.monolith.uk.com
Printed in the UK and USA

Contents

Preface

Local studies collections are rightly seen as unique and distinctive parts of the library and their worth is recognised by professionals and users alike. This volume looks at the impact of the digital age, in particular the Internet, on this distinctive part of the library world. The idea behind this book came from the author's experiences of teaching local studies to Masters students. With each passing year it has become increasingly necessary to revise radically lectures to incorporate more and more innovative and imaginative websites devoted to aspects of local studies.

The work is divided into eight chapters representing broad themes: the background to local studies and the Web, the myth of parochialism, enquiry services, remote users and local materials, e-genealogy, e-collaboration and cooperation, e-learning, and evaluation and appraisal. Undoubtedly, many other aspects could have been selected as the principal themes. However, it is felt that these provide a sound, practical overview of many of the main issues associated with local studies and the Internet. This work is not about digitisation per se; there are no discussions of the technicalities here for there is a vast and more specialised body of literature dealing with this.

The book inevitably focuses on the public library sector as local studies remains a speciality (although not necessarily a unique one) of that sector. Having said this, the importance of other institutions, national, academic and special, is not overlooked.

The book is deliberately geared more towards practical benefit than theoretical discussion. It is not a simply systematic critical review of the literature on the many subjects discussed. Rather, its focus is more firmly rooted in the examination of the issues, problems, concerns and potential solutions of bringing local studies into the digital age. The discussion is based on empirical investigations of good practice and observation of web-based innovations over a number of years within the local studies sector. A great deal of literature has been used during the period of research for this work and one author – Michael Dewe – stands out as being particularly worthy of mention for the impact his publications have had on local studies. His *Local Studies Collection Management* (2002) has indeed had the professional impact and value which is prophesied in the preface to that work.

The selection of examples in this book are based largely on those which have been deemed by the information and library professions as a whole to be examples of good or even best practice; others are included because they offer something innovative or telling or because they fulfil particularly useful functions; some are included because they are 'good' websites. The sample is indicative and by no means comprehensive. The importance of local studies staff undertaking regular and thorough Internet searching cannot be underestimated and is noted at various points in the book. At the end of the day, this is perhaps the most crucial point to get across to those involved in local studies collections management. The best way to develop digital local studies services is to look at what others are doing and to follow this through by thinking creatively about what can be applied to one's own service. Indeed, there can really be no substitute for using the Internet and discovering its potential for oneself.

Peter H. Reid
Aberdeen
June 2003

Acknowledgements

There are many people that I must thank for their help with this book: Mr Alastair Campbell (Libraries Manager, Moray Council) and Mr Mike Seton, Mr Michael Head, Mrs Fiona MacArthur, Ms Kirsten Hume and Professor Derek Law (Strathclyde University). My grateful thanks to those individuals and organisations that have given permission for images of their websites to be reproduced in this book: the staff of Rutland Online; Manchester Archives and Local Studies and in particular Margaret De Motte; Professor Crandall Shifflett, University of Virginia (Virtual Jamestown); the staff at EDINA (Old Statistical Account); Victorian County History Project; the Reverend Susan Wiffin and the Vestry of Gordon Chapel, Fochabers and Major-General Bernard Gordon Lennox; West Sussex County Council Library Service and in particular Ms Sue England; Gateshead Libraries and in particular Mr Peter Bolger; Knowsley Metropolitan Borough Libraries and in particular Mrs Eileen Hume; The Trustees of Genuki and in particular Mr David Hawgood; Docklands Parish Register and in particular Mr James Legon; General Register Office for Scotland and in particular Mr Peter Murphy for permission to reproduce the Scotland's People website; Port Gordon Local History Online; the Public Record Office and in particular Mr Nick Coney for permission to reproduce *Focus on ... The Census*; and Powys County Council and in particular Mr Gavin Hooson (Powys Digital History Project). I am indebted to a number of my colleagues at the Department of Information Management at the Robert Gordon University, Aberdeen. In particular, Mr Ian Johnson, Professor Rita Marcella, Professor Dorothy Williams, Mrs Sarah Pedersen and Mrs Carol Adam. My sincere thanks to Dr Robert Newton for his encouragement and flexibility in enabling me to get out of the office to work on this volume and for allowing me access to his report on Virtual Learning Environments as well as for saving the day when a technological hitch threatened catastrophe. Finally, my thanks to the staff of Chandos Publishing, Oxford, particularly Dr Glyn Jones and Melinda Taylor, and to Peter Williams, the editor.

List of illustrations

List of abbreviations

BAOL	British Association for Online Learners
CILIP	Chartered Institute of Library and Information Professionals
COPAC	Consortium of Online Public Access Catalogues
CURL	Consortium of University Research Libraries
DCMS	Department of Culture, Media and Sport
EARL	Electronic Access to Resources in Libraries
EMOHA	East Midlands Oral History Archive
ERIC	Educational Resources Information Center
FAQ	frequently asked questions
HTML	hypertext mark-up language
ICT	information and communication technology
IGI	International Genealogical Index
IRC	Internet Relay Chat
IT	information technology
JISC	Joint Information Systems Committee
LIBINDX	Library Index (Moray Local Studies)
LTSN	Learning and Teaching Support Network
MI	monumental inscription
NOF	New Opportunities Fund

OPAC	online public access catalogue
OPR	Old Parish Registers
PRO	Public Record Office (now part of the National Archives)
PRONI	Public Record Office of Northern Ireland
URL	universal resource locator
VCH	Victoria County History project
VLE	virtual learning environment
WWW	World Wide Web
WSRO	West Sussex Records Office

About the author

Dr Peter Reid is the Course Leader of the MSc in Information and Library Studies at the Robert Gordon University in Aberdeen, Scotland, teaching both to full-time, on-campus students and to part-time distance learners. His principal teaching areas are in the fields of bibliographic and information sources as well as reference and enquiry services, including local studies. His research interests embrace local studies and local history, digital reference services as well as historical bibliography. His doctoral research examined the history and development of British country house libraries and he has published a number of studies on book collecting of the gentry and aristocracy. He is also a local historian in his home county of Banffshire in the north-east of Scotland and has published local history research both in monograph and web-based formats. He is a Fellow of the Society of Antiquaries of Scotland.

The author may be contacted at:

Department of Information Management
Aberdeen Business School, The Robert Gordon University
Garthdee Road, Aberdeen AB10 7QE, Scotland

E-mail: p.reid@rgu.ac.uk

Introduction

Introduction

This first chapter covers the two core themes of the work – local studies librarianship and digital or electronic developments. Initially, the chapter briefly examines the background to local studies librarianship, addressing the issues associated with the problem of defining what 'local' actually means in the context of the library service, and looks at what subject coverage there needs to be within a local studies collection. Secondly, the chapter moves on to discuss the huge and significant developments in information and communications technologies over recent years and highlight their importance in the context of local studies.

What is local studies librarianship?

Local studies libraries exist in order to recognise the social, economic and cultural activities and achievements of the local community. They exist in order to record, preserve and celebrate these activities and achievements. If the library itself is intended to reflect the entire spectrum of knowledge then the local studies library must be said to reflect the entire spectrum of knowledge within the context of the local community. It is perhaps most succinctly defined by Don Martin writing in *Local Studies Libraries*:

> The local studies service exists to enable members of the local community to define their identity in terms of their own particular situation – family, home, community, region. Collections are established, developed and maintained as public services, in the public interest. The ethos of public service is paramount. The service should form an integral part of the local information network, providing a clearly signposted point of entry to a wide range of local resources. The collections should complement those of other local services, such as archives, museums and local government.[1]

Very often there exists a basic confusion in the minds of the general public (and, indeed, sometimes also in the minds of members of the library profession) that local studies can be equated with local *history*. This is not the case and misrepresents the purpose of a local studies collection which should cover all aspects of the locality, both the physical and built environments, and all aspects of human activity within that locality in the past, present and future. Although originally local studies, in many cases, developed by accident, it is now an accepted and essential part of every good library service, certainly in the public sector and in many cases also in the older academic sector.

However, it would be futile to deny the significance of the role that local history plays in terms of both the subject content and use of local collections. In the past there was a much stronger emphasis on the rich, powerful and grand members of society over the lives of 'ordinary' people. Many local studies collections still, inevitably, retain ponderous volumes on the elite within local society. Local investigation was, in the past, often largely dependent on the educated antiquarians or scholarly clergymen putting together histories of communities and people which frequently focused on the activities of the 'great and the good', often with a notable emphasis on the gentry. Today, however, much greater emphasis is placed on the lives of 'ordinary' people. This change has been one which has emanated very much from the grassroots users themselves. One obvious example is the increased interest in family history.

How local is local?

The first and most important question in terms of local studies is how local is local and how can the local area be defined? This is central to the way in which the collection will be developed and used. It is true that this question is sometimes overlooked because the answer is deemed to be self-evident, particularly in the public sector where the geographic scope and parameters of the collection will, generally speaking, be dictated by administrative or political boundaries. In the academic libraries sector a broader approach is sometimes taken which reflects the traditionally perceived catchment area or the aspects of teaching, learning and research undertaken at the institution. For example, an academic local studies collection might move beyond the simple definition of the county or the shire and cover a whole region such as East Anglia, the Midlands, the West Country or the North-East of Scotland. In the United States the definition might be interpreted as being state-wide.

Sometimes, these geographical or political entities appear to be little more than artificial creations and once probed a little more deeply it becomes clear that communities (often across wider areas which are not necessarily bound together in contemporary administrative terms) see themselves as forming a distinct entity. Such regions might be tied together by a number of different factors which may include common agricultural backgrounds or the existence of particular industries or trades and often by the use of a particular dialect. This latter point is sometimes overlooked and yet is often self-evidently the case. For example, it is true of the north-east of Scotland; the term encompasses four old counties but three modern-day administrative areas which are tied together by the common usage of the Doric dialect.

However, simply leaving it at political or administrative boundaries is, perhaps, too simplistic an approach given the periodic reorganisations of local government that take place. In many respects, the United Kingdom has suffered particularly in this regard with the local government reorganisations of the 1970s and 1990s having shifted a variety of boundaries. The reorganisation which took place in the 1970s saw the disappearance of historical entities like Rutland and the East Riding of Yorkshire. Yet the 1990s reorganisation saw their eventual re-emergence. Even areas which continued to exist often had their boundaries changed. In the 1970s, part of Morayshire in north Scotland went into the Highland region and a large part of neighbouring Banffshire was added to the new Moray district. Consequently, the local studies department had to reflect this by incorporating material on the old county of Banff, while ceasing (at least notionally) to deal with material on that part in the new Highland region.

The cases of Rutland and the East Riding of Yorkshire perhaps signify an important point and one that directly affects local studies provision. The populations of both of these areas retained a strong sense of community identity and belonging even when the political and administrative entities ceased to exist. It is this inherent *localness* that local studies departments seek to foster, reflect and celebrate and it is important that collections reflect this and the communities' perceptions of it. The concept of the East Riding never entirely disappeared despite being subsumed into Humberside for nearly a quarter of a century. Capitalising on this affection for, and attachment to, the area that its people identify themselves with might be said to be the very essence of local studies. Often, however, it is an attachment which goes far beyond the confines of the local studies collection itself. The Rutland Online website emphasises local people's affection for and attachment to their historical county (see Figure 1.1).

Consequently, defining how local is local is not simply about recognising the convenient political or administrative boundaries of contemporary life. As with all aspects of local studies it is about recognising and acknowledging the understanding and expectations of the public. In general terms, this has been achieved successfully in the past with regard to 'conventional' stock acquisitions. However, with the digital revolution it has become potentially much easier to think in broader terms with the ease of access to electronic sources and services concerning neighbouring areas which may still be tied to the community in question by historical, cultural, social or even linguistic factors.

Figure 1.1 Rutland Online

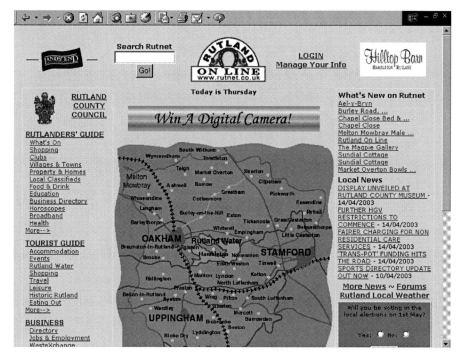

Reproduced courtesy of Rutland Online. Available at *http://www.rutnet.co.uk/*.

Coverage of local studies materials

If one of the most important characteristics of local studies provision is the definition of the local area to be covered then the other must surely be the subject provision to be stocked. Local studies departments should aim to collect comprehensively on local subjects. All aspects of the community and its diversity should be reflected in the stock held. The divisions which information scientists and library professionals create – arts and humanities information, science and social science information and so on – will all be represented in a local collection with that one, overriding qualification: the link to the local area and community. In many ways stock selection for local collections should be straightforward, provided the basic ground rules are observed:

- the topographical definition for coverage is transparent;
- the aim in terms of comprehensive coverage is understood;
- the format of the material is irrelevant to the acquisition.

Comprehensive coverage of subject in local terms must be a fundamental goal for any 'good' local studies department.[2] In an ideal world some mechanism for local legal deposit would exist.[3] However, local legal deposits are complex and, consequently, it is perhaps more important that staff working in this field are able to develop good relationships with local publishers (and often equally importantly local printers) and indeed local authors to ensure that they can obtain copies of all publications relating to the local area. Equally, however, it is vital that staff can access conventional bibliographic sources (and here the Internet proves to be of huge benefit with, for example, online access to sources such as the British Library Catalogue or COPAC (Consortium of Online Public Access Catalogues) in the United Kingdom or the Library of Congress in the United States). This helps to ensure that works produced further afield (but perhaps by local authors) can also be acquired. Local legal deposit schemes should certainly be put in place in terms of the publications (both formally published and grey literature) that emanate from the local authority or parent organisation. In most cases in the public sector this may well be covered by procedures and arrangements involving archives and record offices. Many of these areas of stock acquisition can only be effectively managed if staff act proactively to foster good relations with appropriate organisations and individuals. This subject is explored more fully, in the digital context, in Chapter 6.

Long before the concept of multimedia attained its current status, local studies librarians were adept at thinking in these terms. Collections of local material have always contained a bewildering array of formats from architects' plans to microfilmed newspapers, from sound recordings to weighty genealogical volumes. Clearly, of course, some of these formats require particular equipment in order for them to be utilised. However, format should, on the whole, not be a major consideration in terms of the acquisition of materials. Increasingly, however, attention is turning to the methods of acquisition and preservation of electronic sources dealing with the local community.

The stock of most local studies departments will consist of books (both about the area and by authors from the area), journals, periodicals, newspapers (and most likely also additional miscellaneous files of newspaper cuttings, among other things), photographs (both old and new), slides, films, sound recordings (both musical and voice), maps, plans, charts, drawings, paintings and ephemera. Collectively and in many cases individually, this will constitute a unique resource both in terms of the actual holdings themselves but also in terms of the catalogued records for them.

The use made of local studies departments has increased steadily over the last twenty to thirty years.[4] This increased usage has been mirrored by an increased recognition of the role that local studies librarianship has to play in safeguarding and indeed celebrating local culture, identity and diversity. Hitherto, local studies have been commended for their contribution to collecting and preserving distinct parts of the national heritage with each local area being recorded and documented through the activities of its local studies department. The emphasis has, however, largely been on conventionally published material rather than digital material.

Recent government initiatives focusing on libraries have emphasised their role in delivering social inclusion and lifelong learning. These twin objectives are being addressed at the local as well as the national level and libraries are clearly in an ideal position to facilitate both objectives. Harnessing communities at a local level and providing them with access to information to enable more participative citizenship has become an underlying principle of government policy. It can be argued, of course, that local studies librarianship has been harnessing local communities and providing them with this focus for many years.

Neither of these concepts – social inclusion and lifelong learning – are new to those familiar with the activities of local studies departments. They have always been particularly well-placed for and, it must be said, good at reaching out to the community partly due to the range of materials and partly due to the proactive, hands-on way in which staff often go out into the community. Similarly, lifelong learning is nothing new to the local studies librarian. As Don Martin has pointed out:

> For years they [local studies librarians] have accommodated the expectations of self-improvers working on a variety of local projects, sometimes in the guise of formalized further education, but driven more usually by sheer determination.[5]

Social inclusion and lifelong learning are both dependent on widening access. The concept of widening access to libraries is often taken to mean reaching out to those who feel excluded from society and who may not be patrons of the library. In other words, wider access equals increased *social inclusion*. This is undeniably true and a legitimate goal. However, wider access is a twofold process. Certainly it is about increasing the number of users and facilitating participation by those not previously regarded as users; but it is also about creating wider access to sources and services on a national or even global level. Wider access can therefore be said to be also about *information inclusion*. For existing users (and indeed the new ones too) it is no longer simply a case of relying on the collections within the four walls of the library but rather it is about being part of a much greater network of information sources.

It is this, perhaps more than any other aspect, that has huge implications for the future direction of and vision for local studies services. The essence of this development is that local studies can now go global. With the simple click on a hyperlink, patrons can have access to a vast array of sources available remotely, whether the cataloguing of the Historic Manuscript Commission (*http://www.hmc.gov.uk*) or the digital images of the Hulton Getty collection (*http://www.hultongetty.com*) or the online catalogue of the Library of Congress (*http://www.loc.gov*). Individual local studies departments become links in the chain. Perhaps more than ever the local studies library can, with the aid of the Internet, become a dynamic part of a truly joined-up network of resources. As the next chapter will show, the myth of parochialism has finally been exploded once and for all.

The New Library: The People's Network[6] emphasised the role that local studies librarians have as creators and providers of digital resources. In reality, however, the Internet revolution offers far more opportunities than the relatively narrow confines of creation and provision. Certainly, local studies departments can provide significant and important materials for digitisation and thus ultimately make materials accessible globally. However, it is not solely a question of asking what local studies departments can do for the Internet but it is also a case of asking what the Internet can do for local studies departments. When local studies services do 'go global' through the Internet it is a delicate but vitally important balancing act: giving to the world a taste of the uniqueness of the collection within the four walls of the library while also bringing into those four walls the multiplicity of global resources. It is this balance that is the essence of the Internet.

By all means digitise and diversify but equally importantly the Internet can be harnessed to improve and develop the levels of service provision to users both actually and virtually. The good local studies services will see the need for these aspects to take place in parallel. Dissemination of the service's materials remotely while simultaneously bringing in remote services for patrons is crucial and both are equally important. Ideally, web developments should not just be through a series of bookmarks on a stand-alone computer in the corner of the department but through a fully functioning website available to customers in the library or at home, regardless of whether 'at home' is around the corner or in the Falkland Islands. This is the challenge of the electronic age for local studies libraries.

The Internet

The use of computers in local studies is nothing new and frequently local studies librarians have made innovative advances by embracing new technologies. At opposite ends of the United Kingdom two significant projects were undertaken. In Moray, Scotland, the local studies department introduced the LIBINDX system in the mid-1980s. This system indexed newspaper and periodical articles, photographs, maps, the service's collection of miscellaneous stock, microfilmed Old Parish Registers (or at least those not indexed by the International Genealogical Index) and the library's own card-index of monumental inscriptions for local graveyards. The system is searchable by person, place or subject. At about the same time, a similar system was introduced for the local studies service in Devon which had databases for monographs, periodical articles and images. The Devon system also facilitated the production of an annual Devon Bibliography. Such initiatives often emerged from hybrids of the basic stock control or circulation systems used elsewhere in the library service.

These systems, allied with the provision of other in-house databases very often delivered using CD-Roms, were limited in their scope either to stand-alone computers or to computers networked within one building or, at best, networked throughout the handful of locations that belonged to a particular service or organisation. In the past these technologies seemed to be embraced more eagerly within the academic sector than in the public sector. When they did make their way into the public sector they were often confined to the Reference Department with fewer services in the Local Studies Department. However, as Don Martin points out, 'the local studies service is a core part of the service, and it is essential that this is reflected in library ICT [information and communication technology] strategies'.[7] Increasingly patrons both local and remote expect to see catalogues and local studies indices mounted on the library's website.

The explosion in use of the Internet over the last ten years has sharply refocused this. Indeed, it can be argued that the Internet revolution of the last ten years has been the most important change in libraries since the introduction of the free public library. No part of the library is immune from the changes being wrought by the Internet. These developments have been mirrored by a fundamental shift in the expectations of users and patrons. The Internet alone has not been responsible for this shift but it has contributed very largely to it and has, in many respects, been the catalyst for, or facilitator of, change. Government policies – certainly across the western world – have strongly promoted the electronic provision of information and have strongly encouraged notions of an 'e-enabled' population. As has already been mentioned, two of the most frequently cited themes in the development of this e-enabled population are social inclusion and lifelong learning. Both of these are concepts very familiar to local studies librarians.

Perhaps the first and most important thing to say about the impact of the digital age on local studies is to reiterate that the local studies department is not simply a desirable 'additional extra'; it is a vital core part of the service and, as such, must be an active participant in the developments in information and communication technologies currently taking place within libraries. Additionally, it is essential that local studies departments are properly resourced, both in conventional terms but also in terms of receiving adequate proportions of funding for ICT.

Digital content creation

The New Library: The People's Network clearly demonstrated the importance of this by highlighting the vast potential for digitisation (in its broadest sense) within local studies libraries:

> In local history, above all, libraries house unique collections. Digital technologies will allow such collections to be converted into new formats. This will make these resources more widely available, and their availability in digital format will facilitate security and conservation of the original, often inherently valuable, documents.[8]

Digital content creation is, therefore, out of necessity regarded as the essential first step. Or is it? This work is not solely concerned with issues of digitisation of materials, although this inevitably is a hugely important area. It is equally important to remember the vast array of other digital sources and services (already created by others) which can be tapped into to provide a value-added local studies service.

However, in the first instance it is vital to look at issues associated with digital content creation and certainly libraries need to identify materials they hold that are appropriate for digitisation because, as Nigel Rudyard has said:

> [Digitisation] is arguably the greatest revolution in the dissemination of information since the Gutenberg press, in that potentially it instantly makes available

unique materials to anybody with access to a personal computer and the Internet.[9]

Digitisation of materials is central to this. For the local studies librarian identifying priorities for digitisation, participating in consortia to fund the project and involvement in the practicalities of digital content creation should be becoming part of their everyday duties. Academic libraries tend to have been at the forefront of digitising manuscripts but public libraries have led the way in digitising photographic collections, although this is simplistic because there are numerous examples in both sectors of a wide range of items being digitised.

The reasons behind digitisation would, on the surface, appear to be simple and straightforward – preservation and access. However, it is often seen as a choice between the two. The creation and dissemination of digital surrogates of rare or fragile material is often held up as a preservation panacea. While it undeniably assists in preservation it is not, in itself, a preservation strategy. The question is also posed whether digitisation is done for reasons of preservation or access. It should not, however, be viewed in terms of this polarity. Digital content creation facilitates both. On both sides of the Atlantic equal emphasis has been placed on preservation and access by the (US) Commission for Preservation and Access and the European Commission for Preservation and Access.

What digitisation does is to reduce reliance on perhaps fragile original documents and sources and to enhance greatly the delivery of the material. Taken together digitisation can, therefore, be seen as serving two purposes. What is far more significant, however, is the bewildering array of additional features which electronic delivery can provide for both the actual and virtual user. For example, a collection of digital images accessible on a public library's website can be searched far more efficiently than a filing cabinet of old photographs. There are many excellent of examples of this. One from the academic sector is the digitisation of the photographs of George Washington Wilson by Aberdeen University (*http://www.visual-evidence.ac.uk/aberdeen/controller*) and another in the public sector is the 'Picture your street' section of the website of Manchester City Libraries (see Figure 1.2).

Figure 1.2 Picture your street

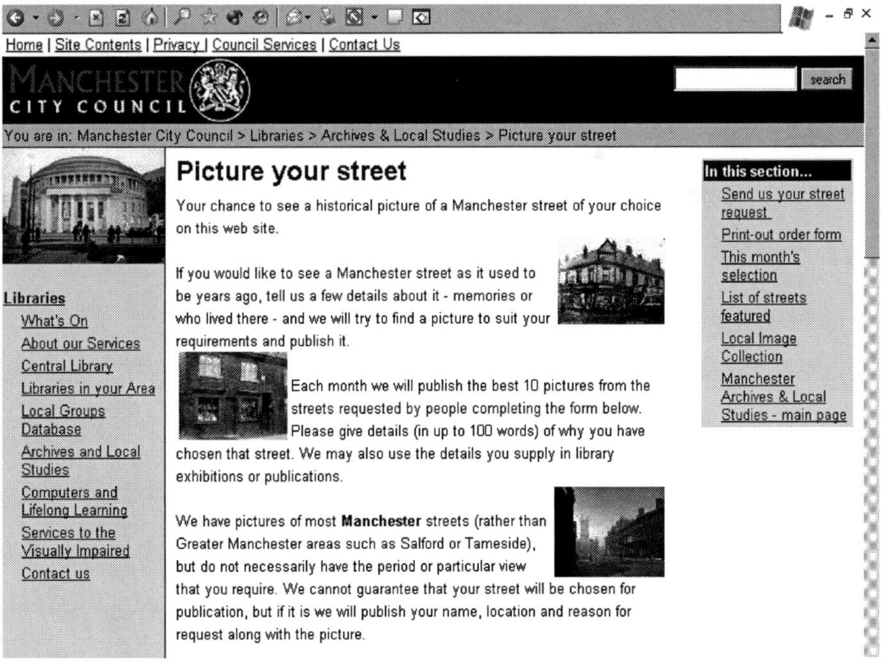

Reproduced courtesy of Manchester Archives and Local Studies. Available at *http://www.manchester.gov.uk/libraries/lsuimage/streetview/index.htm*.

Through such mechanisms it is much easier to provide contextual background to the image electronically and to draw users' attentions to other items which may be of interest. If appropriate research has been done previously it will also be possible to link up to other collections or resources elsewhere. This small example highlights the possibilities which the digital age offers by way of 'joined-up' thinking.

This electronic delivery leads to a perfectly laudable, if somewhat misplaced, assumption that creating digital contents on the Internet automatically promotes social inclusion and lifelong learning. Enabling these twin concepts relies much more on the good, old-fashioned commitment and imagination of the librarian as well. Rudyard also goes on to speak of the importance of what he has described as the 'cross fertilisation of ideas and contents'.[10] This is arguably as important as the primary creation of digital contents, although a great deal of emphasis tends to be placed on the former at the expense of the latter. This book attempts to present a balance between the two.

With so much emphasis being placed on digital content creation it is tempting to consider this to be the principal thrust of the Internet revolution in local studies. The potential that is offered by the Internet to local studies librarianship should be regarded as supplementary to the physical collection. The development of new services which embrace the digital world should not be regarded as meaning the abandonment or replacement of 'traditional' local studies services. If anything, the new media actually strengthen the traditional service by significantly enhancing the outreach capabilities of collection, staff and service. With the Internet has come the ability to reach a much wider audience than has ever been possible in the past. While the Internet possesses an almost limitless capability for dissemination of materials, it would be foolish to suggest that there are not also significant benefits for the patrons who come into the library and use the existing, conventional stock. The cross-fertilisation of ideas and content is, therefore, equally significant.

Global dissemination

However, it is essential to recognise that global dissemination is perhaps the most important benefit of the Internet. With this in mind it is therefore particularly vital that the content creation is well thought through and appropriate and represents what users actually want. There is no point in digitising a seventeenth-century prayer book for the sake of it if users both actual and virtual want something else which is within the library's power and resources to provide.

As the *New Library* report highlights, in local history many libraries hold unique materials and many have identified their local holdings as priorities for the creation of digital content. This means that there is the potential for the global virtual library, one which is open 24 hours a day and 365 days a year. It can be accessed with equal ease from around the corner or from the other side of the world. The Internet means that the unique collection in one library can be easily linked to other, similar collections separated by geography. This is important not only on the global level but also in terms of extending the provision within the local community itself. With significant amounts of digital content (either produced in-house from in-house resources through digitisation or drawing on the materials already provided by others) it becomes possible to extend the service beyond the confines of the local studies department in the central library to outlying branches. This is, obviously, particularly beneficial in remote, rural locations where it may be potentially more difficult for patrons to travel to the central local studies department. Even in instances where libraries have chosen not to provide huge amounts of digital material externally (i.e. on the Internet itself) some have successfully developed intranets which have been extended across all service points. For local studies departments which are generally extremely good at promoting social inclusion, this is obviously capable of presenting new opportunities in the dissemination of materials beyond the central service point.

It is perhaps fair to say that the most beneficial aspect of the Internet – its sheer diversity – is also perhaps one of its biggest drawbacks. This is a failing in a number of significant respects. Firstly, the size of the Internet with billions of web pages means that it is inevitably very difficult to bring any structure to it. The Internet, for all its benefits, is at the end of the day a mass of disorganised, unstructured information of varying quality. Even the best search engines do not make much headway with the Web and statistics for the coverage of search engines vary dramatically. The Internet seems to generate a nagging suspicion in the back of every user's mind – no matter how experienced – that they are missing something and there has got to be more out there. Users also tend to spend a disproportionate amount of time searching for a particular piece of information, spending far more time searching than the end product actually warrants. Ultimately, they often value the piece of information more highly than it deserves because of the length of time – the disproportionately high length of time – it has taken to retrieve it. This is a particular challenge for local studies librarians who must get the potentially obscure noticed out there in cyberspace.

Secondly, the Internet contains much material that is basically of an ephemeral nature which disappears when page authors lose interest or change Internet service providers, leaving no trace but an irritating occurrence in search engines that promises much but fails to deliver. This happens as much with large organisations as it does with private individuals. Libraries are often as guilty of maintaining dead links on their web pages as private individuals who have long since lost interest in the website they created a number of years ago. The ephemeral nature of much of the Internet's contents also poses a significant challenge for local studies librarians because many sites may contain useful records of community activities, organisations, events and even research.

Many local organisations are choosing, quite deliberately, to publish materials on the Internet rather than through more costly short runs of publications. Local historical groups have found publishing details on their websites is often a much more cost-effective way of producing their materials. This poses serious issues for the local studies librarian who must consider the development of a mechanism to ensure that new research which is published electronically can be identified, retrieved and preserved for posterity. These challenges are addressed later in the book.

Frequently, however, no matter how new, innovative or good the digital provision is, the general public still tend to like hard copy. One local author who wrote a short history of his village highlights a common experience:

> Even though the full text of the book is on my website and now freely available for anyone to download, people still want to pay £4.50 for an actual copy of the book which sold its entire print run within about four months.[11]

Methods need to be identified by librarians to ensure preservation of sites likely to be of interest.

Thirdly, and perhaps the most vexing for information professionals, is the quality, validity, authority and reliability of materials that appear on the Internet. The fact that literally anyone can publish materials on the Internet is one of its greatest strengths but also one of its most appalling weaknesses. It results in vast quantities of, at best, irrelevant, inaccurate material and, at worst, rubbish.

Practical concerns

Another issue which must be addressed is the long-term stability of the Internet and the resources which are placed in digital formats. There are unresolved issues about the permanence of the formats used for digitisation of resources, both photographic formats (such as jpeg or gif and so on) as well as for text (such as pdf). Additionally, it is impossible to predict what better techniques and formats may be developed in the future leading to the possible obsolescence of current formats. There have been a number of cases of digitisation having to be redone because the format was inappropriate.

Loading material directly onto the Web may enable global access but it also raises the question of ownership of material once it is in the public domain. Digital content, even that which is copyrighted, can easily be downloaded, altered and passed off as something else. It is a problem that bedevils the education world with numerous sites offering made-to-measure essays or other pieces of coursework. This issue affects libraries no less than any other organisation with an Internet presence. Even text in pdf format can easily be copied. Images are perhaps the most obvious target for copying. There can be few Internet users who can honestly say that they have never copied a picture, very probably copyrighted, from a website. One solution, as practised by Hulton-Getty, one of the Internet's biggest image databases, is to digitally watermark the images, but even this can be eradicated with some creative trimming of the image. If the watermark is placed in a prominent position it is often entirely counterproductive as it can obscure the main content of the image or text and therefore totally undo the benefit of digitising.

These concerns aside, however, the Internet does offer huge potential for local studies collections as the remainder of this volume will show. It must indeed be a significant part of the future of local studies.

Notes

1. Don Martin (2002) *Local Studies Libraries*, 2nd edn. London: Library Association, p. 1.

2. The notion of what makes a 'good' local studies collection is clearly subjective. However, it is interesting to note that while research has been undertaken on what makes a 'good' school library (particularly that done by Dorothy Williams) no comparable investigation has been undertaken into local studies.

3. See Richard Harris, John Feather and Margaret Evans (2000) *The Legal Deposit of Local Publications: A Case Study of Leicestershire, Leicester and Rutland*. London: Library and Information Commission.

4. See Michael Dewe's chapter 'Local studies and libraries', in Michael Dewe (ed.) (2002) *Local Studies Collection Management*. Aldershot: Ashgate, pp. 1–25.

5. Martin, *Local Studies Libraries*, p. 4.

6. *New Library: The People's Network*. Library and Information Commission for the Department of Culture, Media and Sport, 1997 (available at *http://www.ukoln.ac.uk/services/lic/newlibrary/full.html*).

7. Martin, *Local Studies Libraries*, p. 4.

8. *New Library: The People's Network*.

9. Nigel Rudyard (2001) 'Old wine in new bottles: local history in the digital age', *Local Studies Librarian*, 20(1): 2. This is an excellent summary looking both at the broader picture and, more specifically, at initiatives in the north-west of England.

10. Rudyard, 'Old wine in new bottles', p. 3.

11. Private source.

2

Exploding the myth
of parochialism

Introduction

The aim of this chapter is to address the myth of parochialism which is erroneously attached to local studies in general and local history in particular. The chapter addresses how and why local studies have become such an attractive forum for research. It addresses some of the earliest attempts at local investigations and demonstrates how some of these were not at all confined to discrete local areas or communities. It shows how some of the early attempts at local investigation actually provide a much broader picture or perspective on a national or even global level. In doing so, the chapter underlines that local studies do not necessarily equate directly with ideas of local history only. The chapter also seeks briefly to chart the development of local studies collections as part of the library service and to show that, at every stage, strenuous efforts have been made to prevent this from being a purely parochial part of service provision. The final part of the chapter shows that, rather than being regarded as something entirely new and innovative, the Internet is, in fact, just the latest in a long line of methods of popularising and expanding local studies provision. This part of the chapter focuses on web-based resources that have been developed both within and without local studies departments. Various examples of good practice are used to demonstrate how and why the parochialism often attached to local studies is a myth and to examine how local materials have been brought to wider global audiences.

The myth of parochialism

The first chapter in this work highlighted the misnomer that local studies is often wrongly equated directly with local history. In the library context, the terms local history or local heritage collection tend to be applied more commonly in North America although some public authorities in the United Kingdom have opted to use this term as well. Upon the completion of the new Public Library in Elgin, Scotland, Moray Council redesignated the old building as the Moray Local Heritage Centre.

Yet, despite the preference for the inclusive term of *local studies*, many library professionals and library users still regard local history as the primary concern of local studies departments. This is not necessarily a bad thing provided it is done in a creative, imaginative and inclusive fashion and it is remembered that today's current awareness might be tomorrow's history.

To a certain extent, the modern and inclusive notion of *local studies* has suffered from this previous, and perhaps exclusive, interpretation as *local history*. Until the twentieth century, local history (or at least the published outputs of local historical investigations) frequently presented a very narrow and sometimes jaundiced view of the subject. Local history was perceived to be the property of the educated layman, many of whom were gentlemen antiquarians or prosperous clergymen with not too onerous livings to administer. These individuals created what were notionally described as histories of communities but which were, in reality, often more concerned with the history of the church or landownership or, very often, the genealogical pedigrees of the landed gentry. The ordinary man or woman in the street and their experiences were largely ignored by local historians in the eighteenth, nineteenth and early twentieth centuries. Even as 'people's history' became far more common in national or international terms there was still relatively little coverage of it at a local level.

This has, in many cases, damaged perceptions of local studies because it is viewed as narrow, sometimes elitist and ultimately parochial, with little relevance beyond the confines of the manor house or the parish boundary. However, certain qualifications must be made to the criticism of the efforts of past local writers. In most cases, they presented a picture as it would have been interpreted in their day. Their published output was simply a reflection of the fashions of the time. They would not have expected their works to be unsurpassed in the future nor would they have imagined that their own areas of investigation in anyway precluded study of the diverse range of topics associated with the community. The limitations of local investigations, particularly those from the eighteenth and nineteenth centuries, often lie in the fact that they did not have access to the widest range of sources; travel was difficult and archival materials held in a remote location might as well have been totally inaccessible; finding devices to access materials were much less sophisticated and much less widely available and often there was a much greater reliance on access to private sources. Similarly, they did not possess the ability to edit and re-edit their works with anything like the ease of researchers and writers in the twenty-first century. This latter point has often led to the perpetuation of untruths or misinterpretations by subsequent authors.

These earlier studies of county or town, village or parish, estate or gentry should not be underestimated. They often form the core of many monograph collections within local studies and they may very well still be the first sources consulted in a modern-day investigation of a topic. For all their drawbacks, the work of the antiquarians and the clergymen still have a useful role in local historical research.

The grandfather of local studies

One of the most obvious examples of this is the (Scottish) *Statistical Accounts* which saw the clergy called upon to assist in the production of one of the first wide-ranging studies of local conditions. In the late eighteenth century the clergy (in the shape of the ministers of the Church of Scotland) were mobilised by Sir John Sinclair of Ulbster (1754–1835) to assist with the creation of the (first) *Statistical Account* of Scotland. Sir John was an agricultural improver and innovative thinker on rural matters in his home county of Caithness in the far north of Scotland. He also possessed the ability to see far beyond the confines of his own – at that time remote – home. With commendable enthusiasm and even arm-twisting he set about recording a picture of contemporary Scotland at the close of the eighteenth century. *The Old Statistical Account* as it is now known offers a number of important lessons for all local studies collections. Although a good deal of each parochial account was concerned with history (and it was an approach to history that would have not been unfamiliar to most scholarly antiquarians at the time), it also featured a good deal of information on the present state of the country, including industry, farming and manufacturing, and details about the conditions of ordinary people. At the time of its publication, the *Statistical Account* had as much to do with contemporary relevance as it did with historical investigation. Of course, more than two centuries on it has immense historical value (but that was not its sole objective at the time of its compilation). In some respects, Sir John Sinclair is, without him ever realising it, the grandfather of local studies. For those involved in local studies work – and not just in Scotland where the *Statistical Accounts* form a key source – it teaches us the lesson that local studies brought together become a national source because the contemporary description of today becomes the history of tomorrow.

Sinclair's approach was unlike that of the antiquarians of the time who were, perhaps, more concerned with the derring-do of medieval warrior knights. He did certainly include historical details and information about land-ownership but significant amounts of the *Statistical Accounts* are concerned with the contemporary preoccupations of enlightened innovators at the end of the eighteenth century. The entries contain, for example, not just details but in many cases the minutiae of industries, manufactories, mineralogy, trade and educational provision within each of the parishes. Sinclair's *Statistical Accounts* therefore identified that local investigations should be a balance of the historical and the contemporary, something that local studies collections have striven for ever since.

Sinclair realised that by bringing together hundreds of disparate accounts of localities (written by those best placed to comment), he would end up with a picture of the entire country that was of historical, contemporary and future relevance to both those interested in specific localities and those concerned with a nationwide picture. This vision might indeed be an allegory for the Internet today. The idea of providing a national picture through local research was central to the creation of the Victoria County History project (VCH) which came into being at the very end of the nineteenth century. Its goal was to provide histories of the English counties with the recognition that the compilation of volumes devoted to the history of each county would ultimately lead to a much broader understanding both of local areas and, ultimately, of the country as a whole. One hundred years on this huge undertaking is still incomplete.

The writing of local, parochial, urban and, particularly, county histories was nothing at the time of the establishment of the Victoria County History project. If Sir John Sinclair of Ulbster was the grandfather of *local studies* then it is perhaps arguable that another progenitor was William Lambarde whose *Perambulation of Kent* appeared in 1576 and is generally regarded as the first county history. Lambarde might, in some respects, be held to be that grandfather of *local history*. What was new with the Victoria County History was the idea of providing one national series of histories. In the intervening years a large number of more traditional county histories continued to appear and many would have been familiar in their style and format to the antiquarians of the eighteenth and nineteenth centuries. However, a great many other types of county-based studies have been produced often looking at particular subjects or themes – most notably, perhaps, architecture, with works such as Nikolaus Pevsner's *Buildings of England* series or the Royal Incorporation of Architects in Scotland's *Illustrated Architectural Guides* for the counties and districts of Scotland.

Sir John Sinclair was encouraged by the idea that local studies of local conditions can simultaneously be of historical, contemporary and future relevance. Sinclair also realised that while many readers might primarily be interested in their own local area, they would also probably be interested in comparing and contrasting elsewhere and that these discrete local studies can, when brought together, provide a more general picture of a nation. Two centuries on, this is not so very dissimilar from what local studies departments – individually and collectively – are doing. And, clearly, the Internet offers new possibilities by providing a new level of synergy between the local and the distant. There is an irony that something which is so deliberately *parochial* (in the literal sense of the word) as the *Statistical Accounts* actually offers some of the broadest lessons for dispelling the myth that local studies is parochial and insular.

Popularisation of local studies

Local studies have had a long and honourable tradition within the public library sector for over one hundred years.[1] In the first instance, local studies collections tended to be focused more strongly on urban areas. This was inevitable given the mechanisms put in place under the Public Libraries and Museums Act of 1850 for the establishment of public library services in municipal areas. As with many aspects of the early public library service, the emphasis was placed strongly on improvement of the populace. Local collections soon became an accepted feature of a number of libraries and, right from the start, certain broad conventions with regard to local studies were observed, most particularly that the local studies collection was part of the reference library or department. Those running the very early local studies collections were also conscious of the lack of coverage outside the neatly defined boundaries of their town or city and many deliberately sought to acquire materials about neighbouring or surrounding areas. In some cases this was genuinely to create a broader coverage; in others it was to assist in masking the relative lack of material on a town itself. The very genuine ambiguity that still exists when attempting to define what is local often stems from this period.

Inevitably, however, this situation did not ensure anything like universal provision of local studies because many rural areas were still without any meaningful library provision whatsoever. This changed with the passing of the Public Libraries and Museums Act of 1919 which led to the creation of county library services throughout the country. The shire counties thus became able to concentrate the same efforts in services provision as the towns. However, there was a long way to go before any of the rural shires could seriously hope to compete with the large and successful collections in the towns. The Act did, however, mean that these library services could start to collect local materials in a more organised and systematic fashion. Many rural areas that did not include a large town or city within the shire could not hope to rival the collections held in the municipal libraries and, today, some of the biggest and best local collections are to be found in municipal collections such as those of Manchester, Leeds, Glasgow and Edinburgh. However, some rural areas have benefited hugely from the relationship between town and country. The relationship which exists between Norwich and the rest of Norfolk is a good example of this. Norwich was one of the first places to develop a local collection towards the end of the nineteenth century. The Norwich collection has had to recover from a catastrophic fire in August 1994. Yet the model adopted in Norwich of the integration of urban and rural remains a good example. The original 1850 Public Libraries and Museums Act expressed a desire to see the creation of 'topographical libraries' and many local studies collections have emerged from these.

The 1919 Act resulted in many new collections being developed and by the 1930s the concept of local studies as a distinct entity had emerged more fully. In 1932, Edinburgh

Public Library made its local studies collection into a subject department in its own right, a trend that was widely adopted elsewhere in the years to come.

It is sometimes difficult to discern which came first: the wider provision of local studies collections or the increased popularity of local history. What is clear is that the rejection of the labels of parochialism and insularity has not come about on its own. The more organised and coordinated approach to local studies collection management has been accompanied by a growing popularity for local history in particular. Since the end of the Second World War there has been a greater acceptance of the role, function and benefits of local history. Since Leicester University first introduced local history into its curriculum in 1948, a number of universities have followed suit. Hitherto, local history was seen as the preserve of the well-meaning amateur with the emphasis more firmly placed on the word *amateur*. Serious historians examined national and international events, wars and treaties, politics and statecraft. Leicester University and those that followed have rejected this as an approach.

This post-war boom in local history has been mirrored by activities within the library. Indeed, it can be argued that the public library system (and latterly the academic sector too) have been in the vanguard of these developments. In many cases, libraries were actively leading it because, as has been shown, the tradition of seriously and systematically collecting local materials goes back to well before the Second World War. With this increase in holdings has come better organisation of and access to local materials. The technological advances of microform surrogates immeasurably increased access.

Since the end of the Second World War it has become accepted that local studies work is a specialised part of the library and information service in the same way that legal or business librarianship might be viewed. Since W.C.B. Sayers published the first work devoted to local collections (*Library Local Collections*, 1939) a number of important volumes have emerged to assist professionals and students of librarianship understand the common features and issues associated with librarianship. Two contributors in particular stand out. J.L Hobbs whose *Libraries and the Material of Local History* (1948), later reappearing as *Local History and the Library*, and Michael Dewe's *Local Studies Collections: A Manual* (volume 1 1987 and volume 2 1991) and more recently his *Local Studies Collection Management* (2002) have both significantly contributed to the professional's understanding of the collection and, equally importantly, the ethos and management of that collection and, ultimately, its position in the larger picture.

All of this has reinforced the importance of having well-trained staff. In its own way this has helped to remove the parochial stigma as well because these specialist staff members come with a broad understanding of national and local sources and how they interact and relate with one another. Inevitably, these staff members also develop a specific understanding of how unique local sources work. This scrutiny (together with continuing professional development) of the increasingly professional press in the field and attendance at events directed towards local studies staff, has resulted in a much wider perspective being taken; it has manifested itself particularly through collaborative ventures and initiatives.

The parochial and insular view of local studies can be further exploded by looking at who actually uses these collections. In most cases, local studies departments are used by a wide cross-section of the population from schoolchildren to retired people; they have practised lifelong learning long before the phrase became fashionable. This wide cross section of users has resulted in inclusiveness of another kind as well. There is now a definite shift in the subjects being investigated by users and this has led to a much greater emphasis being placed on the lives and concerns of 'ordinary' people as opposed to the once narrow fixation on the pedigrees of the gentry or the topography of the area. This shift in emphasis is one which has emanated very much from the grassroots – the users themselves.

Globalism

There is also a much less tangible but perhaps no less important reason for the increase in interest in local studies and local history. This is associated with the often hectic and perhaps even dysfunctional way in which we lead our twenty-first century lives. Modern life sometimes leads to us being cut off or isolated from our own history and origins. Certainly, nostalgia plays a part in the attraction to local studies but it is often far more than that. The attraction can lie in wanting to possess a 'sense of belonging'. Indeed, local studies – and particularly local studies on the Internet – have been described as attempting to overcome the diaspora away from local communities.[2] It seems somehow paradoxical that as our society becomes more mobile then our need to find out and understand our roots and origins becomes more pronounced. Sometimes this can be associated with naive ideas of halcyon days in a rural idyll but, more often, it is based on a realistic understanding and a simple and perfectly natural desire to know where one comes from both in familial, geographical and social terms.

The role that local studies can play in this need to belong should not really be underestimated. A comparative study undertaken by Céline Ermoin in 1999[3] found that both in Normandy and the north of Scotland, the regular users of local studies libraries and archives possessed a particularly strong sense of local identity and often valued their attachment to their own particular area more highly than their nationality as a citizen of France or Scotland (not to mention of the United Kingdom). The research also showed that these users possessed a much greater awareness of all aspects of local and community life. Their investigations not only resulted in them becoming experts in their own relatively narrow fields but they demonstrated a wider understanding of the culture of their communities as a whole. Interestingly, this sense of belonging demonstrated by the users of local collections also included a particular devotion to the dialect or patois of their particular part of the country, something which has, until relatively recently, been less prominently represented in local collections.

Another reason for the disappearance of the parochial tag is the innovative role of local studies staff; this needs to be added to all of those aspects already mentioned. Over the last forty years the image of local studies departments has been heightened through current awareness schemes, through active involvement with all types of community organisations, through strenuous marketing activities and, not least, through the work of the Chartered Institute of Library and Information Professionals' Local Studies Group as well as through initiatives such as the Scottish Local History Week organised by the Scottish Local Studies Group. Elsewhere, particularly in North America, significant work has been done by privately funded historical societies,[4] either at a state level or in connection with a particular theme, subject or event. In the latter category, the work undertaken by the Valley of the Shadow in connection with the American Civil War is particularly commendable. Similarly, the award-winning Virtual Jamestown (*http://www.virtualjamestown.org/*) presents a digital research, teaching and learning tool devoted to the settlement at Jamestown in Virginia (see Figure 2.1).

Given the recent emphasis that has been placed upon local studies as a rich source of material for digitisation, the Internet can be viewed as another tool for further broadening the frontiers of local studies. Indeed, it can be argued that the Internet perhaps offers the opportunity to remove frontiers altogether. Yet, as the foregoing section outlines, innovation, inclusiveness and a willingness to broaden horizons has always been a central part of the *raison d'être* of local studies departments and, crucially, their staff. Consequently, the

Internet, revolutionary though it undeniably is, should be regarded more as the latest tool to expand collections, services and access rather than something completely different and, perhaps, even frightening.

Figure 2.1 Virtual Jamestown

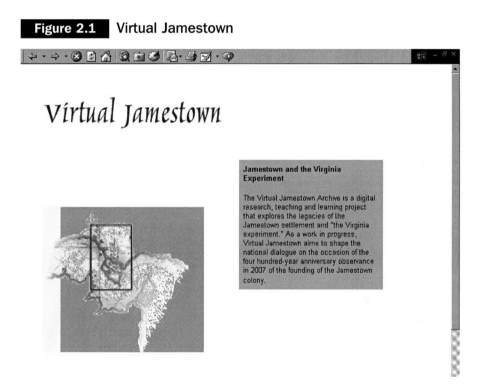

Reproduced courtesy of Virtual Jamestown, Virginia Tech and the University of Virginia Center for Digital History. Available at *http://www.virtualjamestown.org/*.

Digitisation

This work is entitled *The Digital Age and Local Studies.* However, as the preface makes clear, it is not concerned with digitisation itself as a process. A great deal has already been written on both the theory and practice of digitisation in the library context, not least in *Virtually New: Creating the Digital Collection* (London: Library and Information Commission, 1998). Rather, this work is principally concerned with the digital or electronic environment in a more holistic sense. It is intended to provide those involved with or interested in local studies with ideas about how the Internet as a whole can be harnessed to assist with the delivery of local studies services. For the library, the Internet serves two main purposes: on the one hand there is information gathering and on the other there is information dissemination. Allied to this are all the other multifarious uses, for example as an enhanced communication mechanism. This work is principally concerned with gathering and dissemination. In this respect, digitisation forms only a part, albeit an important one, of the relationship between the local studies collection and the Internet.

If, however, the Internet is to be viewed as an additional tool for expanding the horizons of local studies collections then it does become essential to look at the practical aspects of digitisation to a certain extent. Sometimes the role of protector of the collective memory of the local community has been taken very seriously and very literally with little active exploitation of the sources. This is something which *Virtually New* seeks to change. The Internet offers the potential for a much wider exploitation of local studies resources. If one criticism can be fairly levelled at local studies it is that very often they have been extremely good and successful at collection and preserving materials but much more reticent about the possible means of exploiting them either in terms of increased access or in commercial and marketing terms.

Access and preservation are generally regarded as being the two principal reasons for embarking on digitisation projects. On the one hand, the creation of digital surrogates whether on a CD-Rom or on the Internet means that multiple and remote access becomes a real possibility. Electronic dissemination of material means that multiple users can simultaneously consult a particular source, which is hugely beneficial for heavily used items. Perhaps even more important than this is the fact that remote access can be achieved. The inclusion of material on the Internet means that there is as much chance of the user being on the other side of the world as in the next street. If anything this is potentially the most obvious way in which the Internet can widen access to the collection. Elizabeth Melrose writing in *Local Studies Collection Management* (2002) highlights a number of areas that are crucial in any departmental audit and one area that she emphasises is that of access, saying that an audit should ensure that

> access to the collection and the expertise of the staff is made available to as many different sections of the public as possible and whether efforts are made to encourage those who are not using the service at present.[5]

Increasingly, good practice in terms of Internet utilisation is ensuring that this is the case.

The second principal reason for embarking on digitisation is to assist in the preservation of materials. Information and communication technologies offer the potential to offer access to artefacts and documents which are, for reasons of fragility or value or rareness, not normally available to the public at large. In the case of items that are fragile or ones which sustain particularly high usage, digitisation offers potentially significant benefits by enabling the library to create electronic surrogates in exactly the same way as microfilm has for the last half century and thus to protect the physical and intellectual integrity of the original, paper-based source. However, the advantage of electronic surrogates over microforms is, as is outlined in the previous paragraph, the ability to provide simultaneous access to multiple and remote users.

Additionally, given the ever-increasing sophistication of electronic searching techniques, documents which in hard copy required careful reading or endless flicking between index and content can now be searched relatively accurately and efficiently for appropriate references. Even applications as basic as the Control-F 'Find and replace' function in Microsoft products offer a level of rudimentary searching not previously available in hard copy. In reality, it is not simply about making the sources more accessible and available; it is also about making the intellectual content more accessible.

The range of sources made available electronically must also take account of the needs and abilities of the user. As later chapters show, the selection of contents must be managed very carefully and appeal to as wide a range of users as possible. Some materials will be best suited to serious scholarly researchers and some to schoolchildren who may need to know as much about what the source is and how it works as they do the information contained in it. The Public

Record Office[6] has done this very well with its activities for children associated with the Census. Their *Focus On … The Census* site is highly interactive and teaches the younger generation about the importance of the Census as a source and how it works before they go off and try to use it practically. Additionally, it is important to consider the technological issues. Most published works on digitisation suggest that two levels of digitisation are required with higher resolution for archive purposes and a compressed one which facilitates quicker loading. Other techniques such as the use of thumbnail images to enhance loading speeds should also be considered, particularly for pages which contain a large number of images as this will assist those users working remotely through slower dial-up Internet connections.

The link that existed between the local data collection and the broader national picture at the time of Sir John Sinclair of Ulbster has continued to exist and is an important factor in the exploitation of resources. This means that local studies departments can now rely on a vast array of digital sources and services that have been created by national organisations and bodies as well as the materials created at a local level. To a certain extent this has always been the case with more traditional formats but it has, perhaps, become more obvious since the explosion in Internet usage. In some cases, international bodies and organisations can also be responsible for the creation of digital sources and services that are extremely beneficial on a local level, perhaps none more so than the Church of Jesus Christ of Latter Day Saints and their Family Search site (*http://www.familysearch.org*) which provides the International Genealogical Index electronically.

It is satisfying that the efforts of Sir John Sinclair of Ulbster two centuries ago continue to be innovative today and provide an excellent example of how a source can be adapted for electronic dissemination. Given that the *Statistical Accounts* have an important place in the early creation of local studies materials it seems right and proper that it should be available in this brave new electronic environment. It is also reassuring that it has been done so professionally and attractively. The digitisation of the *Statistical Accounts* has been undertaken by EDINA, a national datacentre that exists to provide online services for education and research. EDINA is funded by JISC (Joint Information Systems Committee) and is based at Edinburgh University Data Library (see Figure 2.2). For the *Statistical Account* EDINA has used the original printed versions exactly.

The site provides an excellent interactive interface and offers the user a wide range of searching approaches. The aesthetic appeal of the site is enhanced by the fact that the original has been digitised thus retaining the appeal, formatting and text (see Figure 2.3). A simple rekeying of the text would not have resulted in such an appealing product.

The Victoria County History project has also entered the digital age. However, it is unsurprising given the vast scale of the project that it does not offer the full text of the county histories. Their website does, however, act as very useful promotional and marketing tool and encourages people to get involved with VCH (see Figure 2.4). The website has, if anything, brought the project to a much wider audience.

Figure 2.2 The homepage of the *Statistical Accounts*

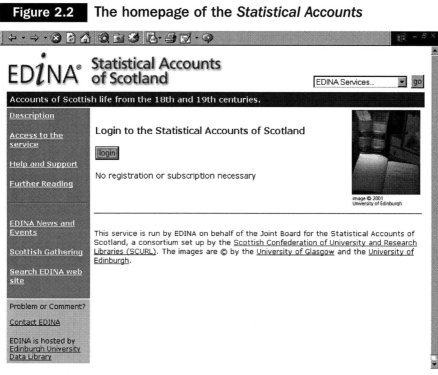

Reproduced courtesy of EDINA. Available at *http://edina.ac.uk/statacc/*.

However, this is not simply a one-way process of national sources feeding down to a local level. The reverse – local sources reaching out to a wider audience – is just as likely to be the case and there are numerous examples of local sources containing essentially local subject matter having direct relevance for other communities on the other side of the country, or indeed the world. A good example of this is the website for Gordon Chapel, a small church in the north of Scotland. On the face of it this may appear to be an archetypal local site about a local organisation. However, the website contains a good deal of detail about the Dukes of Richmond and Gordon who were the local landowners (see Figure 2.5). The Richmond family are based in Sussex and indeed their papers form one of the major collections in the West Sussex Record Office some six hundred miles away. Although in this case this is the website of a local organisation the same can be said of the local studies library.

Figure 2.3 Example of a parish entry from the *Old Statistical Account* showing the description of the Parish of Rathven in Banffshire

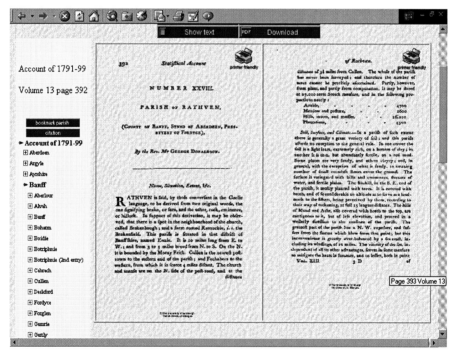

Reproduced courtesy of EDINA.

It is the ability of the Internet to reach right around the world and to attract a global audience, together with the fact that it is a relatively inexpensive promotional tool, that is often the motivation for organisations such as Gordon Chapel to go to the trouble of detailed content creation. Before the advent of the Internet it is unlikely that this type of content would have been available. The Internet has made it possible and made it widely accessible.

Figure 2.4   Victoria County History website

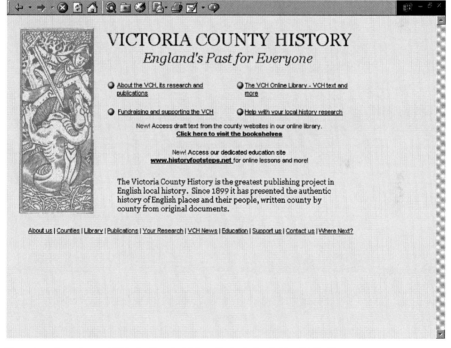

Reproduced courtesy of Victoria County History Project. Available at *http://www. englandspast.net/*.

| Figure 2.5 | Gordon Chapel's web page about the 7th Duke of Richmond |

The 7th DUKE of RICHMOND & GORDON, K.G., G.C.V.O., C.B.

(1845-1928)

Introduction

History

The Windows

Lancets & Rose
St Michael
St Raphael
St Ursula
St Caecilia
The Good Shepherd
St Andrew
Memorial Tablets

Diocese

Services

Events

Contact us

Reproduced courtesy of the Vestry of Gordon Chapel. Available at *http://www.gordonchapel.org.uk/*.

Issues and concerns

The Internet as a whole does offer vast potential benefits to local studies collections and will, in all likelihood, kill off the last vestiges of insularity. However, this may take time and it would be wrong to suggest that the Internet has been universally applauded. Consequently, it is important to attempt to address some of the concerns and reservations that exist about the electronic environment. There are some very natural and very real anxieties which require to be addressed, particularly as they come, in many cases, from professionals within the local studies field. In some sections of the professional community, there is a concern that digitisation in particular is being pursued simply because it is the current obsession of policy-makers and, as a result, obsession together with the availability of funding have conspired to form a vicious circle. Some professionals feel that it is asking many local studies departments to run before they can walk because, as yet, they have not got to grips with the Internet either as a tool for information gathering or as one for information dissemination and that they are being dragged into digitisation too quickly.

More worrying, however, is the fact that there has been concern expressed (although perhaps not always spoken out loud) that many of the traditional elements and activities of local studies departments will be neglected or perhaps even lost altogether in a headlong rush to embrace digitisation. This is much more significant than a more general scepticism about the value of digitisation. Digitisation has never been a panacea and it would be wrong to think of it as such although this rather misguided approach has sometimes been advanced. Digitisation is not without its own problems in terms of the costs (of implementation and replacement of equipment) and staff training and, perhaps more significantly, the fact that it does not in any way alter the need to preserve the original artefacts. It is not, however, a replacement for the original hard-copy collection; it is more a supplement to it and one which enhances and benefits it by increasing access to the sources.

Conclusion

However, hesitation about digitisation should not lead to hesitation about the Internet as a whole and the two perhaps need to be seen separately. A very natural caution does exist about digitisation and its benefits. However, digitisation is only part of an online strategy. The digital age mentioned in the title of this book does not relate purely to a much vaunted idea of libraries creating their own digital content, essential though that will ultimately become. Rather, the digital age mentioned in the title relates to the Internet more holistically. The digital age is as much about the things that the local studies department can *get back* from the Internet as those things it can give to it. So much has now been made available by various organisations and authorities that there are already lots of sources to be tapped into. The arrival of the Internet in local studies departments must enhance the through-the-door visitors as well as the remote ones. This can be done in a variety of ways through electronic sources such as Family Search or the Library of Congress catalogue or through the array of other reference sources that are available electronically.

Certainly, the Internet offers tremendous potential to widen access to local studies and finally to explode that myth of parochialism. Digital content creation offers benefits which are too great to ignore: multi-user access and remote access in particular are significant rewards, while enabling end-users to have access to digital surrogates of rare or fragile material is enormously beneficial. Remote users can access materials and enquiry services can be revolutionised through either e-mail or online enquiry submission forms. The list is endless. Some local studies departments have already created excellent websites that incorporate the local with access to the global but many more sites have little more than a bare outline of what the collection holds. In some cases this appears to mask a reticence about the potential of the Internet. It can perhaps be argued that it is only once there is greater familiarity with the benefits of the Internet that there will be more wide-ranging digitising of collections.

Many of the national bodies in the United Kingdom and elsewhere have suggested for some time that local studies departments should be at the vanguard of digital content creation. Indeed the government through its various initiatives is spearheading this approach. However, many library authorities need to address more fundamental issues first, such as ensuring that local studies are fully integrated into information and communications networks, that they receive their fair share of ICT budgets and that staff are trained to become familiar with and confident about ICT in general and the Internet in particular. As such this book covers some of the approaches that can be adopted to increase familiarity with the Internet and the sources and services it has available for local studies departments.

The spider's web of electronic sources and services that are already available highlights that local studies and their collections are dependent and interdependent on each other and that they are not isolated, insular or parochial. The Internet, the latest weapon for widening the horizons of local studies, offers the potential of collectively creating a vast and accessible archive that not only reflects the memory of one community but of all our communities.

Notes

1. See Michael Dewe's chapter 'Local studies and libraries', in Michael Dewe (ed.) (2002) *Local Studies Collection Management.* Aldershot: Ashgate, pp. 1–24.
2. An idea advanced by Professor Derek Law of Strathclyde University in connection with Glasgow Digital Library Project.
3. Céline Ermoin (1999) 'An investigation into the use of local studies sections and archives and their links with the user's sense of local identity: a comparison between the north-east of Scotland and Manche in Low-Normandy'. MSc dissertation, Robert Gordon University.
4. See P. Sturges and R. Bapty (1991) 'An international view of local studies librarianship', in Michael Dewe (ed.), *Local Studies Collections: A Manual,* Vol. 2. Aldershot: Gower.
5. Elizabeth Melrose (2002) 'Management', in Dewe, *Local Studies Collections Management*, p. 52.
6. As of April 2003 the Public Record Office and Historical Manuscripts Commission were amalgamated into a single organisation, the National Archives (see *http://nationalarchives.gov.uk*).

3

E-enquiry services for local studies

Introduction

The advent of the Internet has dramatically changed the way in which users approach local studies investigation and this is, perhaps, most noticeable in the new methods used to approach and contact local studies libraries with enquiries. As other chapters in this work show, it has opened local studies up to a vast and in many cases new global audience. Inevitably one of the most obvious areas of change has been the advent of e-mail which has, in its own way, made as significant an impact as the invention of the telephone.

The management of reference and enquiry services is a subject which has been investigated by a great many writers. So too has the management of electronic reference and enquiry services. However, relatively little attention has been paid to issues associated with electronic enquiry services within the local studies environment. Yet here, too, the Internet and particularly e-mail has had a very significant impact on the delivery of service. This chapter will therefore examine the issues associated with the provision of enquiry services as part of a web-based local studies service. The focus will be on the practical aspects and the issues surrounding the management of such services (such as the issues for staff and their time). The emphasis of the chapter is on examining both the advantages and disadvantages of electronic enquiry services in local studies. It would be wrong to assume that the brave new world of electronic enquiry services is not without its problems and this chapter identifies them and provides some suggestions on how such problems can perhaps be overcome.

In many respects, the enquiry problems which reference librarians have been familiar with for generations have simply be translated into the electronic environment. Various studies into reference services in general have shown that a large proportion of enquiries by users are inaccurately expressed and it is the job of enquiry staff to attempt to establish, as gently but as efficiently as possible, what information enquirers are really seeking. These issues which have exercised professionals and academics within the reference sector for decades are now also emerging as issues within electronic reference services.

The issues which affect general reference and enquiry services[1] can largely be said to be replicated within local studies too. A number of issues exist:

- users are often intimidated – no matter how friendly and accessible the service;
- users ask general questions that mask their specific information need;
- users ask questions that bear no relation whatsoever to their information need;

- users do not want to appear stupid by asking a 'silly' question.

Added to this, however, are the often peculiar dynamics of local studies:

- users may know (or think they know) a great deal about a particular subject having spent a long period investigating it (this is most often the case with family history but not exclusively so);

- users can be naive about the sources (by adamantly clinging to a belief that there must be another source to prove or disprove their theory or by attaching unrealistic levels of belief in an unreliable source);

- users can often launch into lengthy and complicated enquiries without providing the necessary background or context (this often occurs when they believe that they have developed a 'special relationship' with staff who will remember, in tremendous detail, their particular area of interest);

- new users do not want to show their ignorance of what local studies is all about.

All of these issues have, hitherto, manifested themselves in traditional forms of enquiry, whether face to face, letter or telephone, and now are equally commonly exhibited in electronic enquiries too.

However, there are some additional issues which have manifested themselves with online enquiries. Many of these are associated with the methods used by librarians to guide and direct users to appropriate resources. The creation of detailed guides and instructions to the collection often prevent the librarian being asked a series of mundane questions with monotonous regularity. It is important that such details are also incorporated into the department's web pages. However, it is much more difficult to instil in remote users the idea of being an independent researcher. Staff training is also an issue of paramount importance because online enquiries cannot be answered in the same way as face-to-face ones. In many cases, there is a particular challenge to be faced making local studies staff, who are very comfortable with historical sources, become equally comfortable with modern technological solutions. Additionally, special thought needs to be given to the presentation of findings back to the user where, very often, an e-mail can be used to provide the main facts but supplementary materials (such as photocopies) may have to be posted.

Online enquiry services

There are a number of practical management issues that need to be addressed in connection with online enquiry services. Local studies libraries, whether in the public or academic sectors, will be subject to performance measurement associated with response times to enquiries in exactly the same way as the reference department itself will be. These response times must be applied equally to the electronic environment too. However, local studies departments tend to receive a higher proportion of enquiries from outside their own geographic area from individuals who are not contributing (through local taxation) to the maintenance of the service. Methods for dealing with such enquiries need to be in place because this is one area that will certainly increase as soon as electronic enquiry services are put in place. Equally, some of the enquiries that are received by local studies departments are particularly complex and may involve staff undertaking a lengthy investigation.

This complexity of investigations has led to many libraries introducing commercial rates for longer pieces of research. These rates often apply in the reference department as well as in the local studies department. Many local studies departments have reached this situation after learning some hard lessons about the commercial value of their services and the skills of their staff. For example, in the past, local lawyers may have used the local studies department and their staff knowledge and expertise *for free* perhaps in connection with a property sale, but then the law firms have added a charge for 'research' to their client's bill.

There is a wide variety of different techniques in operation across the library sector for charging. Some services do not charge at all but prefer to limit the time spent on a particular enquiry. This is not, perhaps, the most satisfactory approach because an additional hour might just reveal the answer to the enquiry and the client might be perfectly prepared to pay a commercial rate to obtain the information he or she seeks. Those services which do charge use a variety of different approaches. Some libraries do not charge for the first hour of the research then charge a commercial fee for every subsequent hour spent on the investigation. Some choose only to charge for photocopying and other materials. Some authorities will give priority to enquiries from residents within the area (i.e. in the public sector, the taxpayers who pay for the service) and will not charge for them while making a charge for those outside the area.

If commercial fees are introduced for local studies searching by staff then the costs need to be clearly shown on the website. Consideration needs to be given to the mechanisms by which users can pay for this (credit cards, cheques, postal orders). Increasingly, it may become necessary for enquiry services to offer these financial transactions online because the pressure for this exists among user groups. If that is the case, then it becomes an issue of e-commerce and one that extends beyond the library itself to those responsible for the website and the server. Ultimately, this may become a decision for the parent organisation and they will need to ensure that their server is secure for online business transactions and that suitable software is in place. However, this is an area of development that local studies departments may well have to get involved in as many of the national agencies are increasingly (and successfully) offering purchasing transactions online. Prominent among these are the Public Record Office (now part of the National Archives) or the Scotland's People website both of which enable users to purchase online credits to enable them to search particular sources (such as the Census or Statutory Registers of Births for example). Access to the United Kingdom Census online is managed in a similar fashion.

Libraries do, however, find themselves in a quandary with online enquiries (and indeed with remote enquiries in general, irrespective of whether they come by telephone, mail or electronically). Many remote users will contribute nothing to the library itself while those users actually within the building may well, through their local taxes, pay for the service. Balancing services to remote patrons with those for patrons present in person is potentially difficult and without easy answers. While there is evidence that charging makes users value the service more it does raise questions about social inclusion and, particularly with the advent of the Internet, about dealing with international enquiries and the general inconvenience of foreign currency transactions.

E-mail enquiries

By far the most common method for providing some form of online reference and enquiry services is through the use of e-mail. Since the mid-1990s e-mail has become a central feature of most organisations' day-to-day existence. Many local studies departments report that the level of their enquiries has increased (in some cases quite dramatically) through the introduction of e-mail. As with all enquiries, whether received through the post, by telephone or through e-mail, they can vary from the simple and straightforward to the complex and time-consuming.

Treating e-mail enquiries in the same way as those that come by letter is not without dangers. It can be argued that e-mail has, to a certain extent, fostered a culture of impatience, perhaps even petulance. The immediacy of e-mail is one of its biggest benefits yet for the recipient it can be one of its biggest drawbacks. E-mail often heightens the expectations of the user because it is simple and quick to use and leaves the user feeling that they have immediately achieved something. This sense of immediacy tends to mean that the user expects a very quick response from the organisation that they are contacting. Some techniques (including Internet Relay Chat, discussed later in this chapter) deliberately foster a culture of immediacy but, in many cases, e-mail enquiries are often treated no differently to postal ones and are subject to the same prioritising for response.

Given that many users maintain a somewhat unrealistic expectation when it comes to e-mail, it is therefore important that the enquiry page on the service's website outlines clearly the standard response time for the enquirer. However, many enquirers will largely ignore this on the website so a better mechanism (and one which is available in a large number of e-mail software packages) is in the shape of an automated response whereby an automatic acknowledgement of the receipt of a message can be issued. This can be tailored to the service in question, stating (for example):

> We acknowledge receipt of your enquiry to the Local Studies Department. We aim to provide you with a response in x days.

The factor x can be determined by the policies of the library or its parent organisation. Providing this sort of automated response mechanism can go some way to prevent the enquirer firing off a truculent e-mail of the 'I sent you a message two days ago and you still haven't replied' type. It may, however, be necessary to get back to the enquirer earlier if the enquiry turns out to be complicated and requires protracted investigation. Their willingness to pay for the research (if a charging mechanism is in place) must be ascertained before embarking on a more lengthy investigation.

From the perspective of the user (and particularly the remote user), e-mail enquiry services offer a new and more convenient mechanism for gathering information. Family historians have not been slow to seize upon the potential of the Internet although, to a certain extent, local and community historians have been somewhat more reserved in their embracing of cyberspace. The genealogists in particular have quickly seized upon the benefits of being able to e-mail questions or queries across the world to local studies departments that will be able to assist in their quest to uncover their family history. E-mail, therefore, offers more immediate access for remote users who may often feel disadvantaged in their quest for, say, family history if they are living at the other side of the country, or indeed the world.

Ultimately, electronic enquiry services are about widening access and diversifying the service for the benefit of users and about providing them with an additional contact mechanism. Although e-mail can be said to 'e-enable' new audiences to a certain extent, it can also be a double-edged sword. The ease with which e-mails can be dispatched may mean that once the first e-mail is answered there then follows a barrage of supplementary ones asking a variety of progressively more complex questions. This possibility highlights the need for local studies departments to teach the basic skills of researching local subjects so as to enable users to become independent researchers. This is something which local studies departments have always been good at for those visitors to the library itself. It is, however, less easy to achieve with remote users.

There may well come a stage when the e-mail enquirer cannot be assisted any further. This points to the fact that it is vital that online enquiry services are thoroughly integrated into the other parts of electronic service provision including online subject gateways, newsgroups or more generally available Internet sites. It is important, therefore, that local studies staff are very familiar with the Internet as a resource and can search it quickly, easily and efficiently. Extensive use of bookmarking of sites is vital and the ability, within an enquiry response, to suggest other websites to consult gives the impression of an e-enabled and professional service. Perhaps the majority of these bookmarked sites will have a subject focus but it is equally necessary for librarians to seek out and appraise those which assist in the process of creating independent researchers. Consequently, it is useful for librarians to identify websites which provide details (from the basic to the more complex) about searching the Internet (and there are no shortage of such sites). Additionally, it is useful to have links to, or bookmarks for, guides (either in-house or external) that teach basic information literacy and research methods for local investigations in particular. The inclusion of such sites in an e-mail enquiry response create, in the minds of users, the impression of a value-added service.

E-mail enquiry services are clearly not without their problems. To a certain extent many of the issues outlined at the commencement of this chapter can be said to be replicated in the electronic environment. However, e-mail enquiries bring their own peculiar issues as well. Many users of e-mail regard it as much more informal than a conventional letter. This often leads to enquiries being expressed poorly or inarticulately, lacking clarity and detail. The librarian must be conscious of this and be tactful when seeking clarification. One of the negative points of e-mail is the fact that sometimes it is necessary to indulge in a brief e-mail correspondence before the exact nature of the enquiry can be pinned down. The problems identified at the beginning of this chapter about the ways in which clients seek information can become exacerbated in the electronic environment. Nor is e-mail a very good mechanism for conveying nuances of tone or, indeed, of individual style; something may be meant to be taken humorously but can end up giving offence (on either side). In general, attempts at humour using e-mail should be avoided. Misunderstandings often occur through the use of e-mail and there is the ever present danger of sending the wrong e-mail to the wrong person with disastrous results. There can be the frustration of dealing with 'mailbox full' or 'undeliverable' messages and the consequences of these when the user finally sends another message demanding an explanation for not having received a reply to their enquiry. Yet there is no other method by which the enquirer can be contacted. It is important that staff are not overexposed to e-mail enquiries. E-mails can become relentless and a system which was intended to make communication over great distances easier and faster can become burdensome, even tyrannical. Dealing solely with online questions or queries can become monotonous and a balance with face-to-face users and their enquiries should be encouraged.[2]

The librarian may also find themselves in the position of having a series of regular e-mail correspondents who feel that they have struck up a particular friendship. In such circumstances, the e-mails may end up being not so much about locating the user's great-grandfather in the 1861 Census as finding out what the user's grandchildren did on their summer holidays. This is a difficult situation for library professionals to deal with. The friendliness with which a librarian approaches enquiries is absolutely central to good enquiry practice but a line has to be drawn somewhere. To this end, it is advisable to have general e-mail addresses, such as *localstudies@libraries.oldtown.gov.uk* rather than an address for a particular named individual such as *john.smith@libraries.oldtown.gov.uk*. By providing a general address rather than a specific one for an individual the user has no guarantee that their enquiry will be dealt with by the same person so helps avoid the inclusion of extraneous details. A general e-mail address also provides for the capacity for e-mails sent to it to be opened by more than one named individual ensuring continuity of service if one person is on holiday or away from the enquiry desk. However, in such circumstances it is important to ensure that a mechanism is put in place to log e-mail enquiries and to ensure that two members of staff do not end up working on the same enquiry.

Online enquiry submission forms

Increasingly, a large number of public authorities are providing to users, through their websites, the opportunity to complete an online enquiry form. West Sussex Libraries, among others, has introduced this system (see Figure 3.1). West Sussex's approach is commendable because it demonstrates a joined-up approach to reference, local studies and archive enquiries. Their website encourages users to ask reference questions. The general reference questions option is open only to residents of West Sussex; users from further afield are directed to the national Ask a Librarian (*http://www.ask-a-librarian.org.uk/*) service. The West Sussex site encourages inclusiveness because it has an additional section geared directly towards responding to children and their enquiries. In addition, as Martin Hayes, West Sussex's Local Studies Librarian, outlined in his article 'Sleeping with the enemy', the West Sussex Local Studies Department and the county's Record Office have developed a close working relationship and this is evident from the approach taken on their electronic enquiries web page:

> The Library Service is able to provide information about the printed and microform sources we hold. We answer specific queries which take up to half an hour. If your enquiry is more complex, the West Sussex Record Office offers a comprehensive and fee-based research service.[3]

| Figure 3.1 | West Sussex Libraries Local Studies and Family History Enquiry submission form |

Contact Us

To send us your general comments about any aspect of the Library Service or your thoughts on our website, just fill out the form below and click 'send'.

If you have a reference question or a local studies query, click here to use our 'Ask a Librarian' service.

Data Protection Act - please read before completing.

*Please note, fields marked with an asterisk are compulsory

We welcome your comments..

We are constantly reviewing our services and would appreciate any suggestions you may have to help us plan for the future.

Title: Mr

First Name:

*Last Name:

Age Group: Under 10

*Email Address:

Postal Address : (For administrative purposes and postal delivery of answers, if needed)

Postcode:

My Local Library is: Please Select

Comments:

© West Sussex County Council Library Service, 2003. Available at *http://www.westsussex.gov.uk/ librariesandarchives/libraries/contactus/home.htm*.

Internet Relay Chat

Internet Relay Chat or IRC has become a very popular mechanism for communication with chat room facilities available on a variety of different sites, most notably perhaps through the search engine Yahoo! (*http://www. yahoo.com/*). In recent years a number of libraries have adopted IRC as an additional mechanism for reaching out into cyberspace. Libraries in the United States have been using such technology for sometime and it has become increasingly common in continental Europe as well. In the United Kingdom, adoption of IRC has been slower with fewer libraries readily embracing this approach. Gateshead Libraries in the North-East of England have, however, adopted this approach for their reference services.

As an electronic enquiry technique, Internet Relay Chat is well suited to quick reference enquiries that can be easily answered from one or two sources or from a quick Internet search. Equally, it is particularly suited for referral enquiries, especially those that involve directing the user to various web-based sources. Its application in local studies enquiries is perhaps more questionable. Given that many local studies enquiries involve the protracted consultation of a wide range of printed and other sources it is perhaps less easy to see how the immediacy of a technique like IRC can be harnessed in the local studies context.

Gateshead Libraries have implemented Internet relay chat on their website using their ASAP system (see Figure 3.2). However, this system is associated with their general reference service provision and not with local studies. Live chat mechanisms such as this does, however, require there to be a member of library staff sitting logged into a terminal at all times. Most libraries are not in a position to offer this service 24 hours a day, seven days a week, although in the United States this has indeed happened. Gateshead, for example, operates during normal working hours. IRC does have one significant advantage over e-mail and that is in fostering the idea of having an immediate dialogue with a real person at the other end and doing it in real time. It is, however, an area that remains to be exploited within a local studies context.

| **Figure 3.2** | Gateshead Libraries ASAP Live chat service |

Reproduced courtesy of Gateshead Council. Available at *http://www.gateshead.gov.uk/livehelp/open.htm*.

Frequently asked questions

A central but often overlooked part of any electronic enquiry service should be the provision of a section dealing with frequently asked questions (FAQs). The inclusion of FAQs should be done overtly and certainly it should be prominently advertised on the service's website. If, for example, an online enquiry submission form is available then a link from that page to the FAQs should be made. Indeed, it is eminently sensible to encourage users to look at the FAQ section before submitting an electronic enquiry.

For the local studies department, an FAQ section should attempt to serve two distinct but interdependent functions. In the first instance, it should attempt to answer questions about the extent and scope of the collection and services. This should not, however, simply be a bland outline of the types of stock held (although this can certainly play a part). An FAQ section should go further and actually answer the types of questions that users are likely to have both about the collection and the subject coverage as well as what types of service are available. The creation of this type of FAQ site should not be particularly onerous or time-consuming as all of these questions will have been asked in the past and their answers will be well rehearsed by library staff. In many cases, the information will often have been provided in hard-copy leaflets that the department has produced to explain itself to users. The simple transfer of such leaflets onto the Internet does not work particularly well because their appeal is lost when they are no longer sheets of neatly folded A4 paper. If this is the case, then it makes perfect sense to extract the information and upload it electronically in a much more user-friendly question-and-answer type format for viewers in cyberspace.

Secondly, however, it should actively address examples of the type of 'real' questions that are directed to the department. By doing so this may help to overcome some of the concerns that some new users may have about asking 'silly' questions that betray their ignorance of the subject or the purpose of the local studies department. This is a sound approach and will assist in putting users (and particularly young ones or those with no previous experience of using the service) at ease.

In terms of both the collection and the subjects, a good range of exemplar questions and answers should be selected. These should range from those that can be answered with a few words to those that have perhaps taken more prolonged investigation and require to be explained with a few paragraphs of text. This should, of course, be mixed with those enquiries that are most frequently asked. It may well be that some of these turn into frequently asked questions about particularly famous local events, people or places. It is a good idea to include, at the beginning, some of the 'stupid' questions that users might be shy about asking.

Sharing responses

Maintaining details of the enquiries that are answered electronically is absolutely essential. This need not, however, simply be a passive archive that can be accessed only by library staff because there now exists a variety of techniques whereby this type of material can be actively shared with users. On a general level, maintaining an electronic archive of enquiries can serve two purposes. Firstly, it can be used for the gathering of statistics and for analysis of the types of questions that are being asked frequently. This may lead to additions to the FAQ section or to the production of new information leaflets or web pages if one or two subjects are appearing regularly. Secondly, the electronic archive can be called on subsequently to provide an answer or partial answer by means of 'cutting and pasting'.

Some may regard 'cutting and pasting' as unprofessional. However, it is pointless to unnecessarily research a question which may have already been investigated.

Cutting and pasting responses depend on a number of factors, not least that the e-mail archive is well organised. Staff should always attempt to provide a descriptive subject heading to e-mails so that the Sent box can be easily searched. This highlights the fact that little things can often make a big difference. All too often it is easy to click on 'Reply' without changing the Subject box. This inevitably means that the Sent box becomes full of e-mails with the heading 'Enquiry' rather than 'Worthing Railway Station in 1900'; the latter is obviously going to be of more help in the future when dealing with another request for information about that subject.

Weblogs

Weblogs can be described as being web-based diaries maintained and regularly updated either by an individual or by a team. Again, Gateshead Libraries have been at the forefront of developing reference weblogs in the United Kingdom. Indeed they have established the first weblog in a public library (see Figure 3.3).

The types of postings made on the weblog can vary dramatically. However, many local studies enquiries are not particularly well-suited to inclusion on a weblog. Genealogical enquiries stand out as being most unsuitable for a weblog because of their volume and because of their highly specific nature. A weblog made up of genealogical enquiries would, very quickly, end up looking like a discussion thread on a site such as GenForum.

Figure 3.3   Gateshead Libraries weblog

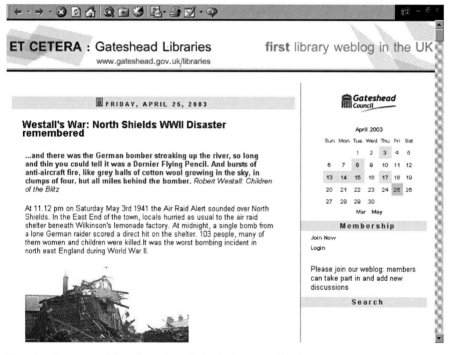

Reproduced courtesy of Gateshead Council. Available at *http://refdesk.weblogger.com/*.

However, virtually all other types of local enquiries can be loaded into a weblog very efficiently and effectively. A particularly worthwhile use would be uploading responses to enquiries about a particular place or event. Indeed, maximising the wealth of research that might otherwise lie dormant in an e-mail Sent box and placing it on a weblog could be entirely beneficial.

Bulletin or discussion boards

Another interactive technique which can be applied is the use of a bulletin board or discussion thread. These can be used to encourage users to post messages and to enter into an interactive dialogue with other researchers. Bulletin boards or discussion threads can be used by users who wish to get in touch with others interested in the same subject or place or to post enquiries that the library itself cannot respond to. In addition, users very often find excellent websites and other resources that the librarian, for whatever reason, has not been able to identify. Sometimes these are peripheral sites (for example, a user may have identified an excellent website which enables the conversion of the historical values of currency into its modern-day equivalent) but, nonetheless, this may be of help to other users. It is necessary, therefore, for local studies staff to monitor these systematically and draw on the resources. As with enquiry analysis, a regular demand for a particular subject or category of information may lead the library to attempt to address this in some fashion. Some of the websites identified on bulletin boards by users may be added to the FAQ section or the links section of the website. Equally important, however, is the need for monitoring to ensure the removal of any inappropriate or offensive messages that may have been posted.

The adoption of bulletin boards or discussion threads needs to be carefully managed. The scope and remit of such sites needs to be clearly identified to users so that they are aware that by posting on this site they are looking for advice, support or assistance from *other users* and that this is not part of the library enquiry service. Nevertheless, these interactive approaches have become immensely popular tools as sites such as GenForum can testify and it is an area which local studies departments would be well advised to consider adopting as another means of reaching out into the community – in this case, a wide and inclusive virtual community with much expertise and many talents.

Staff training

In general, the Internet has brought a number of unresolved training issues for staff within local studies libraries. These are visible in all contexts of local studies work but perhaps most obviously within the context of enquiry services. In some respects users have led this with the Internet becoming their preferred tool for family and community research; many users are more familiar with electronic and web-based tools than are the library staff. This imbalance needs to be redressed with very systematic Internet training for local studies staff. This requires a two-pronged approach. Firstly, it requires staff to have the abilities to seek out all of those local sites which, if they were conventional publications, would have been deposited in the collection (or at least, strenuous efforts would have been made to secure deposit). Secondly, it requires staff to be familiar with the broader range of sources available over the Internet, both those focused on local studies subjects such as genealogy or community history but also with the information tools such as the major search engines and the online bibliographic databases and catalogues.

Nicola Smith has said that:

> ...the most important ingredient of a successful enquiry service remains a well trained and enthusiastic staff, working in a well organized and welcoming library. Local studies librarians need to take basic library skills and apply them within the local studies collection.[4]

This is undeniably true but a qualification needs to be added. Local studies staff also have to become familiar with the particular, not to say peculiar, dynamics of dealing with remote enquiries delivered online. In particular, staff need to be aware of the immediacy that remote users often expect and also, significantly, that electronic enquiries cannot necessarily be responded to in exactly the same way as a letter or telephone call. The ability to include a file attachment explaining a particular point or the inclusion of a website address or a digital image in the e-mail response to an enquiry can make a good service become an excellent one in the minds of users.

Conclusion

With the increased emphasis on the use of information and communications technologies within local studies departments, it is inevitable that the number and range of enquiries received electronically will continue to grow. The point, made elsewhere in this book, that the growth in ICT has been mirrored by the growth in interest in the areas that local studies deal with will also contribute to the expansion in remote enquiries.

Given the dilemma that local studies departments face in providing a service to remote users who are not contributing to the collection or to its financial upkeep, other mechanisms need to be considered. One mechanism may be the inclusion in all e-mail responses of a request to these remote users to consider depositing a copy of the outcomes of their research in the library. It may not be payment for the use made of the service but it may provide the library with some tangible and beneficial end product. Even if these remote users only supply a URL for their web page this can contribute to the development of the collection.

Ultimately, it may not be possible for every local studies collection to endorse all of the techniques and technologies but, equally, they cannot be ignored either. A number of factors need to be addressed by library managers, not least the management of electronic enquiries (and in particular remote users) and the training of staff to ensure that the experience of the electronic enquirer is every bit as good as that of the face-to-face visitor.

Notes

1. Nicola Smith provides a very good overview of local studies enquiries in Michael Dewe (ed.) (2002) *Local Studies Collection Management.* Aldershot: Ashgate, pp. 153–64.

2. The present author, in his duties as Course Leader for a distance learning Masters programme in Information and Library Studies deals, on average, with over three thousand e-mails a year from students and would, by his own admission, go mad if this were not balanced by face-to-face contact with on-campus students.

3. *West Sussex Libraries and Information – Ask Us* available at *http://www.westsussex.gov.uk/Li/askus/home.htm.*

4. Nicola Smith (2002) 'Enquiries', in Dewe, *Local Studies Collection Management,* p. 163.

Remote users and local materials

Introduction

The aim of this chapter is to address perhaps the most difficult, but ultimately the most important, issue associated with local studies and the Internet: namely, the types of materials that can and should be provided electronically to remote users. Inevitably, an examination of what should be made available electronically will also look at the issues that are associated with providing greater levels of access for users. The chapter presents a discussion of the practical considerations of the types of materials which should be made available electronically by drawing on examples of current practice. The chapter does not focus upon the technological aspects of digitisation and content creation. A great deal has been written on this and a wealth of information, both practical and theoretical, is available for those who wish to pursue these aspects.

A great deal has been written about virtual, digital or electronic reference services. However, reference sources, whether they be electronic or conventional hard copy, have always been geared towards a wider appeal – basically to as many reference departments as possible. The vast array of reference sources that exist are there to provide responses to particular information problems, whether they be quick reference queries or long and complicated literature searches. The dynamic is very different within local studies. Certainly the goal is to enable users to find an answer or a response to their particular question or problem but the same universality of sources simply does not exist across the board within the local studies context. It is the individuality of local studies collections that makes them so important. Each individual collection has the capacity, if not always the ability, to provide access to a unique range of holdings; there exists the potential to create digital resources made up of materials that cannot be accessed in any other way beyond the narrow geographical confines of the 'local area'.

The Internet provides an opportunity to create a genuinely 'joined-up' approach to the delivery of local history. However, it is undeniable that some local studies professionals remain sceptical about the purpose of electronic dissemination and are, perhaps, unclear about the benefits of it. Local studies, as has been shown earlier, form a dynamic part of the library service and the Internet offers the potential to develop the service in a variety of exciting and challenging ways. Some libraries have seized this opportunity; Knowsley Library Service in the north-west of England has created an award-winning local history site which draws heavily on its local and archive collections. The reasons for this development were simple:

The creation of software versions of our existing local studies and archive collection will allow us to evoke and interpret the past in a format relevant to today's audience.[1]

Evocation, interpretation and relevance to the audience of today can indeed be said to be three worthy outcomes and may serve well as objectives for other libraries considering the creation of digital content using their local studies collections.

Local studies without walls

At a very basic level, the mounting of local studies materials on the Internet can result in overcoming one of the most difficult aspects of local studies: the location of the physical collection. Ironically, both sides of the location coin tend to create problems not only for local users but also remote ones. In many instances, the local studies collection may be located solely in one library – very often the main central library for an area. This can often lead, particularly in large and sometimes remote rural areas, to a suspicion that the county town or main centre of population gets all of the resources and benefits and that outlying parts of the community are neglected. Coupled with this is the fact that this may also alienate users within the local community who find it difficult to travel to that central location.

Conversely, the other side of the location coin can also present difficulties as well. Some library authorities have neither the space nor the resources to house their local collections together. It is often the case, particularly in densely populated urban areas, that the local studies collection may be split between two or even more libraries. In some academic collections this also happens because the focus may be on providing subject libraries or departments which has the result of dispersing the local collection into a number of different locations.

As has been mentioned elsewhere in this book, the development of digital content enables materials held either centrally or disparately to be brought together to provide a universal point of access to the collection so that users in one building can easily gain access to some of the materials held elsewhere and remote users with hitherto no access at all can now benefit from parts of the collection. Perhaps the greatest single benefit of the Internet is, however, the ability to reach a much wider audience anywhere in the world. The creation of digital content is not simply about enfranchising members of the local community but is also about enabling a much wider audience to share in unique local resources.

Content selection and creation

Once the decision has been taken to create a website incorporating elements of the local studies collection the first and arguably most important question which requires to be addressed is what to include. When beginning to consider the content creation for a local studies website it is important to recognise that the website must be as socially inclusive as possible and must reflect the community as a whole. Social inclusion is not some trite, politically correct term for reaching out to the disadvantaged within society; rather it means reflecting each part of the community equally. This means that industrial history and agricultural history are of equal worth, that the rich in their mansions and the poor in the terraced houses are equally important and that each town, village and parish has a contribution to make.

Generally speaking, there are two sorts of local studies websites. These may be characterised as either (a) *informational* or (b) *interactive*.

Informational websites are basic and modest in their scope. At best they act as online finding aids and at worst appear like badly compiled lists. Many local studies departments have opted to provide little more on their websites than a brief outline of the type and range of materials that are held by the library. They do, perhaps, include some images from the collection but beyond this the site is purely informational. Such sites often give the appearance of having as their sole objective a desire to increase the number of remote enquiries or to encourage people to visit the collection itself. Many collections, particularly in the public sector, have local studies websites which are basically modest lists of holdings. They do suggest some wonderful and unique resources but these have not been exploited. Frequently, local authorities do not have the resources to create dynamic and interactive websites. However, equally often, imagination and drive are also lacking.

Interactive sites, on the other hand, go much further and attempt to provide the story of the area in words and pictures and much else besides. These websites are not simply concerned with informing about the collection but are equally interested in informing about the area. Through judicious selection from the local studies collection the content of these websites is both informational and interactive.

Good practice: Knowsley Library Service

Those embarking on the creation of a website drawn from their local studies collection could do no better than to look at the experience of Knowsley Library Service which, in 1998, launched one of the first interactive local studies sites in the United Kingdom. Knowsley, located on the outskirts of Liverpool, is a metropolitan borough made up of nine townships. The development of the website was made possible with financial support from the Department of Culture, Media and Sport and the Wolfson Public Library Challenge Fund. The objective of the project was to develop the service's information technology and its education role. The library service, in partnership with part of the Computer Science Department at Liverpool University, had just three months to create the site. The result was the development of a vivid and imaginative local history website which remains an example of good practice for the rest of the local studies community (see Figure 4.1). In its first six months online, the Knowsley Local History site received more than 75,000 hits from all around the globe.

The Knowsley site is particularly successful on a variety of levels. Firstly, the content which the site includes has been judiciously selected and attractively presented. Secondly, it recognises that it is serving at least two different audiences – local users who may be very familiar with the area being

Figure 4.1 Knowsley Local History website

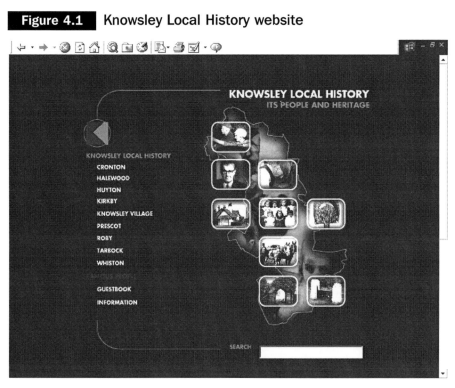

Reproduced courtesy of Knowsley Metropolitan Borough Council. Available at *http://history.knowsley.gov.uk/.*

covered and remote users who may or may not have any particular knowledge of the district but who are attracted by the quality of the presentation of materials on the website. Consequently Knowsley can be classed as an interactive site but also one which is conscious of the other main distinction which needs to be borne in mind when considering local studies websites, namely that there are also two distinct categories of users – local and remote. In this respect, the Knowsley site offers a number of lessons for others considering following suit. The site always manages to inform one category of users without ever patronising the other. The content is accessible and understandable without ever being simplistic and the visual appeal of the site encourages users to continue to explore it further.

Although the Knowsley site was set up with the local community in mind as the primary audience, it was careful not to define the local community as being only library users (or, more particularly, local studies collection users). The educational value of the site was considered from the outset and the benefits to local schools and their students was uppermost in the minds of those responsible for content creation. Encouraging and fostering new users must be seen as a crucial element in any local studies website.

Consequently, it is important to emphasise that the successful local studies site will be one which attaches as much attention to the attraction of non-users from the local community as it does in appealing to the seasoned users. In terms of the local communities that the library is serving, a good local studies website should whet the appetite and strive to encourage non-users to visit. An essential part of any local studies website should be a thorough explanation of all the types and categories of resources available in the collection as well as the provision of details about how to use local history resources. One of the criticisms of the creation of local studies websites is that they may not actually encourage users into the library. The creation of an attractive and informative site may well interest people surfing the Internet and may delight local residents but, in itself, it may not actually encourage them to make use of the collection. As no local studies department will ever manage to make everything available electronically, it is essential, therefore, that websites emphasise that the materials available electronically are just the 'tip of the iceberg' and that a wealth of other material is also available. Guidance needs to be provided in order to assist new users delving into community or family history for the first time.

Content creation: the practicalities

There are a number of points that need to be considered before the process of content creation should be started. As has already been mentioned, it is important to ensure that the site is socially inclusive. Although this phrase is often taken to be related to ethnic diversity or financial position it is, in fact, far broader than this. There is a tendency to concentrate on a few aspects of local history, either in terms of subject or location. This is an ironic position to take as most local studies collections will have material that represents extraordinarily broad coverage of the community and its collective memory. Social inclusion in the context of content creation should, therefore, be taken to mean that all parts of the (geographical) area represented within the collection are represented equally.

The subject content of the website should, ideally, represent the best of the collection without allowing one or two areas to dominate the coverage. It is important to remember, however, that quantity of material does not equate with quality. Having a wealth of conventional sources on a particular topic does not necessarily mean that it should have the greatest coverage on a website which must attract a multiplicity of users with very different and diverse interests. It is important to bear in mind that some types of sources (particularly monographs) simply do not translate well onto the Internet. Town and country, city and village must be represented equally. No one area should be given preference.

Similarly, it is not enough to base the site entirely around a representation based on geography alone. A thematic approach is also required – looking for example at agriculture or industry, education or housing throughout the entire area. The site should not be principally focused towards the approach of one type of local historian. Community history is not all about conducting investigations in a town, village or street; rather, it is often about underlying themes. A local studies department is just as likely to attract enquiries from someone researching coal-mining in the area as they are to receive enquiries about the history of a particular village.

The importance of presenting a balanced approach was recognised during the creation of the Knowsley website; each of the nine communities within the Metropolitan Borough with their own unique and distinctive characteristics have been given equal importance. The Knowsley project team also saw the thematic approach as being crucial, not only in bringing local history alive for a contemporary audience but also because it is so obviously allied to the importance of providing efficient and effective mechanisms by which any interactive site can be searched or interrogated by users using keyword searching.

Providing a balance in terms of the subject and geographic coverage is, however, only part of the balancing act that requires to be undertaken when creating local studies websites.

It is important to ensure that there is an appealing balance of text and visuals and, whenever possible, the two elements should be tied together as tightly as possible. It is necessary to exercise a degree of care in the selection of text. It is preferable that text for a local studies collection website should be created *specifically* for that website rather than culled from other documents which potentially risk alienating users by the inclusion of inappropriate materials. There is often a laudable desire simply to replicate an obscure or forgotten text from the nineteenth century about a particular aspect of the community's history. However, this is frequently a dangerous strategy because the text may not be suitable for reproduction on the Internet; it may go into inordinate detail in language that is inappropriate for creating a culture of accessibility. In most cases, it is far better for the librarian to create the text themselves, synthesising information from a variety of sources and pitching it at a widely accessible level. Local studies sites that work well are ones which are not overburdened with long textual discussions. Care should also be taken that a balance of text is presented within the various sections of the website. Little things can have a significant impact – the choice of font, the size of text, the length of paragraphs, the register used all play a part.

If a section can only enable a few lines of text while other sections have a few pages then consideration should be given as to whether or not it is worth including it or whether it can more usefully be merged with another section. Users can get alienated if the site seems to promise more than it actually delivers. Conversely, choosing to include a section simply because there is a great deal of information available is not necessarily without risks either. Users become alienated by sites which require lots of mouse-clicking (so avoid single pages with four lines of text and a picture). Equally, however, they become annoyed with sites that have page after page of unadulterated text that seems too vast to read. It is easy for webmasters to fall into the trap of saying that users 'can easily print it out if they are interested'; many users may not have access to a printer and their curiosity may wane well before they find the nugget of interest that is relevant to them and their enquiry.

One accusation which has been levelled at local studies collections (particularly those in rural areas) is that they contain a disproportionate amount of material on the rich or grand landowning families within the community. The ducal family in their castle nearly always generated more material than the impoverished in the workhouse. Yet this is an inevitable consequence, not least because the eighteenth- and nineteenth-century scholarly antiquarians – in many ways the progenitors of the whole concept of local studies – tended to have a much deeper fascination for the 'great and the good' over the 'ordinary and humble' (apart from anything else the 'great and the good' were often their patrons providing the financial backing for the production of the multi-volume histories of the nineteenth century that local studies *habitués* are so familiar with).

There might be relatively little information on the workhouse but it might, perhaps, be of greater interest to a contemporary audience; the information on the ducal family might be immense but of less interest to a modern-day audience. Yet the duke and the pauper are both equally valid. Disproportionate amounts of sources on the shelves need not be replicated on a website. Yet this dichotomy is not without its dangers. Firstly, it might be that too much emphasis will be given to the ducal family and their exploits simply because there is a vast array of material on them. Alternatively, the ducal family may be largely ignored in an exercise in politically correct inverted snobbery. Neither approach is appropriate for a website which must represent the community as a whole.

To see how this should be handled effectively, it is useful to turn again to Knowsley where this balancing act is managed particularly well. Within the boundaries of the borough can be found Knowsley Hall and its estate, the ancestral seat of the Stanley family (the Earls of Derby) who are arguably among the grandest of the grand. Knowsley's website handles coverage of the Earls of Derby in a lively, informative and accessible fashion (see Figure 4.2). The coverage is enhanced by pictures of members of the family and a virtual tour of the estate and the Hall. It never underestimates their contribution to the community but nowhere on the site are other inhabitants of the community short-changed at the expense of the Stanley family.

This example is, of course, only indicative but, ultimately, even the best local studies websites are only indicative. The challenge lies in ensuring that the indicative sample of materials that is selected for inclusion provides the best possible showcase for all that the collection has to offer to a wide and diverse range of users that is no longer restricted to those in the streets around the library but is potentially anywhere in the world.

Figure 4.2 Knowsley Local History website, page on the 17th Earl of Derby

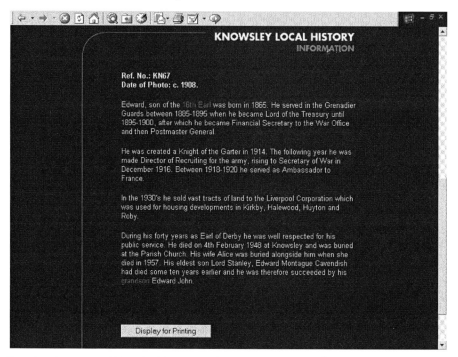

KNOWSLEY LOCAL HISTORY
INFORMATION

Ref. No.: KN67
Date of Photo: c. 1908.

Edward, son of the 16th Earl was born in 1865. He served in the Grenadier Guards between 1885-1895 when he became Lord of the Treasury until 1895-1900, after which he became Financial Secretary to the War Office and then Postmaster General.

He was created a Knight of the Garter in 1914. The following year he was made Director of Recruiting for the army, rising to Secretary of War in December 1916. Between 1918-1920 he served as Ambassador to France.

In the 1930's he sold vast tracts of land to the Liverpool Corporation which was used for housing developments in Kirkby, Halewood, Huyton and Roby.

During his forty years as Earl of Derby he was well respected for his public service. He died on 4th February 1948 at Knowsley and was buried at the Parish Church. His wife Alice was buried alongside him when she died in 1957. His eldest son Lord Stanley, Edward Montague Cavendish had died some ten years earlier and he was therefore succeeded by his grandson Edward John.

Display for Printing

Reproduced courtesy of Knowsley Metropolitan Borough Council. Available at *http://history.knowsley.gov.uk/*.

The interactivity of the Internet is perhaps one of its greatest strengths. The Internet enables users (regardless of whether they are local or remote) to interact more fully with their subject and the sources available to study it. Very often it is difficult for all but the most seasoned users of local studies departments to understand how and why all the disparate array of sources fit together. The Internet offers an opportunity to provide a joined-up approach which easily ties together the various different kinds of sources. Street maps can be linked to old photographs, the buildings might be linked to old valuation rolls, the occupant's obituary from an old local newspaper might be added, audio interviews with older residents of the street or village might also be included. The possibilities are, indeed, limitless. Contemporary images can be added to create a 'past and present' facility, and links can be added to websites for local organisations.

Developing such levels of interactivity also offers local studies departments another significant opportunity. It can enable them to nail the stereotypical lie about local studies departments and their collections that they are 'boring' places full of 'old things' (possibly both the sources and the users). Often this lie is perpetuated by local studies websites which are purely informational, providing nothing more challenging than a list of the categories of sources available to users who actually choose to visit the collection in person. Consequently, the inclusion of the quirky or the humorous, the anecdotes and sketches cannot be regarded as dumbing down but rather is emphasising the diversity of the collection and broadening its appeal – and, not inconsequentially, showing that local studies and local history is indeed interesting and, quite possibly, even fun.

Engaging with the audience in this way is obviously central to the creation of a good website. The potential distinctions in categories of users (local and remote) and of non-users has already been highlighted. However, it is important to consider the sub-groups of users who are likely to be attracted by local history sites. Prominent among these are children and young people. For a website to appeal successfully to this audience, bombarded as it is with a plethora of interactive multimedia, it will be necessary to provide them with entertainment as well as education (even if that entertainment is carefully disguised learning). The potential offered by these sites as educational tools is discussed in the chapter on e-learning. However, it is important to consider this aspect within the context of content creation. Ultimately, it is the relevance and attractiveness of resources that help foster links between local studies and the education system. A very clear link has always existed between local studies collections and the education system at all levels but this has come into much sharper focus since the digital explosion of the 1990s.

> With the emphasis of the [UK] national curriculum on using primary sources, school children who need to find out about, and make use of, the materials will benefit from the use of information technology and digitizing to make a range of documents available. Also, a well-designed, graphical presentation provides for a more stimulating experience for young people.[2]

This highlights the fact that the uses of the site (in this case for the purposes of teaching and learning) should be core to the types of materials included and the ways in which that material is presented to users.

There are a great many other examples of local sites, some developed by libraries and some by heritage groups or organisations. In the United States, the Folkways Montana Heritage Project (*http://www .folkways.org/*) has highlighted some of the benefits that can be obtained from the online delivery of local history material within the context of education. They point out that schools gain quality teaching resources (including photographs, maps, digital copies of primary materials, letters, journals and newspaper reports) thus enhancing the learning experience for students. The school students then become more engaged with their families and community. The educational community (both teaching staff and students) clearly see the learning potential of modern technologies (an inevitable corollary being that they become familiar with transferable skills which will serve them well in later life). Finally, students, by participating in projects which will ultimately become online resources themselves, begin to understand better the contribution that everyone can make in the study of local subjects. This final point offers all involved in local studies websites one further key lesson which is, perhaps, best articulated by Folkways itself:

> All members of the community are transformed into experts on something. Since family history and community history are often synonymous, parents and grandparents have been valuable sources of information about the past. Anyone may become a source of information about a community's history, folkways, science, geography, built environment, or culture.[3]

The creation of a local studies collection website is clearly about choosing materials that are informative, visually attractive and well-presented; it is certainly about ensuring that all interests are reflected equally and that the intended audiences are all catered for (both the local user who can actually go to the library and access the collection as well as the remote user who cannot). However, it is also about stimulating the user. If local studies collections in general are about enabling individuals and groups to develop and, in many cases, to disseminate their contributions to the collective memory of the community then local studies websites are about e-enabling communities by marrying the past with the present. Consequently, electronic content selection and creation needs to stimulate interest and, equally crucially, nurture the often hidden talents of users to enable them to realise that they too have the potential to make a contribution to their community. In this way, the Internet has the potential to become a very powerful tool to facilitate social inclusion.

An A to Z of content creation

There are certain fundamentals that are to be found on almost all local studies sites whether they are informational or interactive. These fundamentals tend to be text (often drawn from a standard, well-regarded local volume), photographs (invariably old ones) and cartographic materials with a wide range of other sources being called on sporadically, even sparingly, on most sites. Very often these three fundamentals are adequate. However, in cyberspace there are billions of plain 'adequate' websites and, given that one of the huge attractions of local studies collections tends to be the wide range of sometimes quite unorthodox source materials, clearly an opportunity exists here for local studies departments to seize and develop innovative content.

The whole notion of A to Z (or even atoz) has become popular with the explosion in the use of digital resources. It may be argued, with some justification, that it is often little more than a gimmick. The following A to Z is by no means comprehensive nor is it definitive and it is certainly far from being incontestable. It is, however, intended to provide those embarking on the creation of a local studies website with some helpful suggestions and useful ideas about aspects that should be considered.

A is for Audio. The inclusion of audio materials should be considered. Some local studies departments have long viewed oral histories as important parts of the collective memory of the community. Many people would never dream of writing down their memories of places, people and events but will happily speak into a dictaphone and to reminisce orally. Organising this can be time-consuming and may not be something which a librarian would want to be involved in directly. However, very often, this is something which local heritage societies and organisations will eagerly and actively participate in and frequently, because of their grassroots appeal, they have a better chance of getting 'good' recordings from interesting people. One such example comes from Scotland, where a heritage group, conscious that the local fishing industry was in decline, set out to record the experiences of as many retired fishermen as they possibly could. Twenty years on, the result is an important oral archive which is begging to be placed on the Internet.

Internet technology is now such that short, edited reminiscences about places, people and events can easily be uploaded and equally easily listened to by users given the variety of multimedia packages that are now available. Relatively few local studies sites have embraced this technology as yet. Many local studies websites have details of their oral history archive but these largely tend to be informational with few including audio clips which can be accessed using software such as Real Player or Windows Media Player. This situation is due in no small part to the fact that, unlike the simple creation of webpages, this is a more complex, time-consuming and costly process requiring a higher level of expertise. No public authority is likely to be able to match the audio archives provided by commercial providers such as the History Channel's archive of famous speeches (at *http://www .historychannel.com/*). However, the inclusion of audio materials does add a great deal to a local site.

Southampton City Library is one authority which has loaded audio clips onto its site (*http://www.southampton .gov.uk/leisure/oralhistory/*), essentially as a means of advertising the oral history archive rather than providing mass online dissemination. However, it is an interesting example and includes the reminiscences of a survivor of the *Titanic* and the memories of someone who grew up in the Southampton Workhouse in the early twentieth century. More could be done, however. As early as 1984, a survey showed that almost 40 per cent of public libraries were involved, in some form, in oral history.[4] Many libraries, such as Bradford, Nottingham and Southampton, have been actively involved in oral history and many organisations, such as the East Midlands Oral History Archive (EMOHA) or the North West Sound Archive, exist to further this aspect of preserving the memory of the community. Digital dissemination is surely the next step.

B is for Books. Monographs may well be the mainstay of many a local studies collection but they are perhaps the least likely to be included (or at any rate, included successfully) on a collection's website. Nevertheless, there should always be interaction between the electronic and the hard copy. This can take a variety of different forms. In the first instance, the published literature should be drawn on for basic text during the content creation stage. There is the temptation with content creation for cyberspace to think that everything has to say something new and innovative, even in local studies. This is not the case and there exists the opportunity to breathe new life into perhaps long forgotten works by citing them or quoting from them on the website. Often obscure gems can be reinvigorate by this approach. A nineteenth-century volume, for example, can still offer the definitive description of a particular place, event or person and should therefore be used in content creation (gazetteers are particularly good in this context). This may well lead to a renaissance for the source and a rekindling of interest in the place, event or person. Interaction with the hard-copy stock should also be provided on the site by the inclusion of further reading lists on particular topics or themes. The possibilities here are endless – it may be the inclusion of bibliographies on a particular place or subject or general titles relating to family history or local history in broad terms could be provided with links to an online bookshop, whether the library itself or a commercial vendor such as Amazon. However, the delivery of full-text books through websites is not particularly satisfactory. Quite apart from the issues associated with copyright (see below), there are a number of reasons why book texts should not be included on websites, ranging from scanning difficulties at the creation stage to ergonomic issues associated with reading on screen at the dissemination stage, not to mention the difficulties in selecting appropriate items. The exceptions may well be the traditional, short, paperback books that are often the mainstay of local history publishing, the older of which may be out of copyright.

Another exception is the books that have been produced by library themselves. These may include 'Past and Present' type works which show photographs of a particular town or village historically and contemporaneously with minimal accompanying text. For those which are out of print and are no longer considered commercially viable for a reprint, consideration should be given to mounting them on the website either in html or pdf formats.

Another area where books may well form an important part of the website is in terms of providing an online bookshop facility. Many local studies departments offer local publications for sale as part of their service. In some cases libraries will simply be convenient outlets enabling local authors to sell their publications; in others the library may, in fact, be responsible for the creation of the work through their own in-house publishing schemes; in others the library may have provided small grants to individuals or organisations to produce short print runs of a work on a local subject. This is certainly an area that could be developed within a collection's website. This may vary from relatively sophisticated e-business sites which are capable of handling secure credit card transactions or it may simply be providing details on how to order by telephone or letter.

C is for Copyright. The issue of copyright of material is, perhaps, the most important single consideration when embarking on digital content creation and must be thoroughly investigated at the outset with appropriate legal advice sought if necessary. However, the copyright of many of the items included on a website will, in fact, be held by the library itself. This might include many of the photographs and certainly the text of information leaflets or current awareness bulletins.

D is for Digitisation. Since the potential of the Internet was first realised, digitisation has been an area which has much exercised the information profession. Hitherto much emphasis has been placed on the digitisation of materials within academic special collections. However, since the advent of the *New Library* much more attention has been turned to the digitising of materials within the public sector. Local studies departments are rightly seen within this context as being important repositories of materials. This book has never sought to be a manual or textbook on the practical or technical aspects of digitisation per se but it is important to reinforce here that the digitisation of materials is central to the impact of the Internet on local studies collections. It is important to realise, however, that digitisation of historic resources is not the only issue associated with the electronic delivery of local studies services. There is an undeniably huge potential in this field and current projects have hardly scraped the surface.

E is for Ephemera. In many respects, ephemera are particularly suited to being digitised because the material is often not lengthy and in many cases makes for attractive web pages. All sorts of ephemera may be uploaded onto the Internet. One of the very best examples of a digital emphera collection has been undertaken by the Glasgow Digital Library project which, in 1999, collected political pamphlets and election leaflets associated with all those candidates and parties standing in the Glasgow and West of Scotland constituencies during the first election to the Scottish Parliament. The materials included in the digital archive might otherwise have been lost or disregarded as being inconsequential. Already, the resource is being actively used by researchers.

F is for Family History. As Chapter 5 dealing with e-genealogy outlines, family history is tremendously popular and is often the main reason for a large proportion of users coming into the local studies department. This scenario is, therefore, likely to be replicated with the local studies website with a large number of users of the website probably being interested in pursuing their family history. Many local authorities have created very good sites outlining genealogical provision.

In the first instance a site examining the genealogical provision should include details of holdings within the library and easily accessible links to those outside organisations (family history societies or registrars) that may have additional materials. Linking to sources such as Family Search or EARL's Familia (*http://www.familia .org.uk/*) is essential.

G is for Guestbook. Guestbooks are not simply part of the natural evaluation process but they are also a very effective mechanism by which researchers can get in contact with one another. As Chapter 5 on e-genealogy shows, discussion threads have become hugely popular within that sphere. It is therefore desirable for local studies sites to embrace this facet of website design.

H is for Help. The nature of help facilities on a local studies website is not the same as that provided on, for example, a database or piece of software.

In the first instance, many users will have a particular and specific enquiry which requires a member of staff to reply. The website will never be capable of containing answers to every question. Consequently, as Chapter 3 on e-enquiry services demonstrates, it is important to have an obvious mechanism by which staff can be contacted (and, additionally, the service should have targets in terms of how these enquiries will be dealt with). The inclusion of a frequently asked questions (FAQ) page may well avoid staff time being taken up providing needlessly repetitious responses to particuar questions.

A log of enquiries received through the website should be maintained. If particular questions seem to be coming up again and again then this, perhaps, points to the need to modify the site. Such questions may be factual ones or they may indicate that users are having a particular difficulty finding material within the site. In either case, a log of enquiries can be viewed as the first step to remedying this.

The log might result in the inclusion of more questions in a FAQ section or it may, as is increasingly happening, result in the creation of a dedicated weblog section within the website where all enquiries and their subsequent response can be mounted for other users to view and, if need be, to react to. Significant developments have taken place with regard to weblogs in recent years and a number of public and academic libraries have successfully integrated them into their e-reference provision.

I is for Interaction. The more interactive a site is the better. Users like to feel that sites are inclusive and participative. This relates not only to games or quizzes or the ability to fill in forms online or to provide feedback but also to the fact that the site must be responsive to their particular needs. However, younger users are particularly keen to see genuinely interactive elements included. Very often the highly interactive elements are something that the organisation creating the site feels uncomfortable with and, perhaps, feels unable to deliver on their own site.

However, the systematic searching of the web and linking to other, well-established sites can serve a useful purpose. *Focus On ... The Census* is perhaps the obvious and best example. It provides interaction and teaches users about the Census at the same time.

Judicious selecting from the rest of the Internet is vital. All sites should attempt at all times to engage with their users in cyberspace; they should not be elitist; they should not simply be long lists of bland information. Whole new virtual communities are being created and increasingly many of these have a very sophisticated understanding of the Internet.

J is for Job. For any local studies website to work and work effectively and efficiently it must be seen as a core activity. It must be viewed as a central part of the job, not simply the job of the webmaster or the local studies librarians but all of those who work in the collection. The site is not something that once created can be forgotten about it. Rather it is an ongoing and living project. Consequently, individuals needs to have the time and resources to make it work.

K is for Kids. Saying that children are the future not just of local studies but of the entire library service may be a cliché but providing material likely to appeal to them is essential. Local studies departments have always been good at reaching out to the younger members of the community because of the link between education and local history. While 'catching them young' does not always lead to them becoming 'good' library users there is a clear need to provide stimulating materials for younger users.

As Chapter 7 on e-learning outlines, a number of highly successful and individual projects (such as the Powys Digital History Project) have recognised and tapped into the wealth of teaching resources available in local studies departments and archives. Many local studies staff have developed close relations with teachers both at primary and secondary levels and, thanks to the hard work of both sides, the resources of the library feed into the curriculum both directly and indirectly. Providing material electronically not only enhances access to the community at large but it positively attracts and encourages children, many of whom will be more familiar with ICT than their parents.

Even when it is difficult for a library to mount materials of its own (for financial or other reasons) the ability to link to remote resources elsewhere is obviously one of the great benefits of the Internet. The ease with which links can be made to other organisation's materials means that some genuinely interactive and kids-friendly material can easily be included. *Focus On ... The Census*, produced by the United Kingdom Public Record Office (now part of the National Archives), is perhaps one of the very best examples of this. Perhaps more than any other site this enables children to gain a thorough understanding of what the Census is all about while also having some fun. Yet this site, which is both a teaching *and* a local history resource, is one which relatively few local studies department have linked their own websites to.

L is for Links. It is vitally important to think carefully about the quality of the links provided on the site. Links should be made to sites that will appeal to and assist both the local and the remote user. For example, if a particular street is being portrayed either in text or in images then appropriate links could be made to the Census. On the one hand it should be possible to open up a new window to tell users of the website what copies of the Census are available to them if they visit the library. Additionally, however, a link could be made to those agencies which can provide remote electronic access to the Census.

Regular checking of these links may be a chore but it is an essential one. Nothing is guaranteed to annoy and put off users more than a site inhabited by a series of dead links and error messages. It is therefore essential to consider, right at the outset, what strategy can be put in place to ensure that hypertext links are regularly reviewed and kept up to date.

M is for Maps. The inclusion of maps (subject to copyright clearance) should be seen as an essential element within any local history website. Maps, both old and new, are a wonderful resource and their highly visual appeal makes them particularly suitable for inclusion on the Internet. Equally, there is an inherent fascination for old maps of local places and this appeal works on a number of levels across virtually all user groups and subject areas. There is a universality to cartographic material. One of the benefits of uploading maps on the web is the ability to create a 'spyglass' mechanism to enlarge maps to the next scale or to link between old and new. The Knowsley website uses the 'spyglass' mechanism very effectively and, as in so many other areas of local studies websites, this is a good model.

N is for Newspapers. Old newspapers have long been one of the principal attractions of local studies departments. They record historical events on an ongoing basis and, very often, can supply details on particular events that are recorded nowhere else in print. Most libraries have local newspapers available in microfilm format. The digitisation of local newspapers is one area in which there is particular scope for collaborative ventures given that the appeal of the newspapers is likely to extend beyond one discrete local area. Digitisation is, however, only part of the process and much time and effort also needs to be attached to creating suitable methods by which they can be searched.

O is for OPAC. Whenever possible, local studies sites should include a link to searching the online public access catalogue (OPAC) for the library. Many libraries will have some local materials duplicated in lending stock and there is an inevitable overlap between local studies materials and reference materials (particularly but not exclusively in the field of biographical information). It is highly desirable for local studies sites to tap into other collections and use links to enable users to access other online catalogues. Neighbouring local authorities should be incorporated into the site because, as Chapter 1 outlines, the geographical boundaries that define local communities are never particularly clear cut. It is also particularly useful in many circumstances for academic libraries to be brought into the picture as they can often interpret their 'local' collection in wider terms than, say, public authorities.

Additionally, the older universities, because of their history and development, may have a range of older sources (including archival materials) that cannot be accessed elsewhere. The ability to search the archive collection for the authority should also be included, ideally in a single searching interface.

P is for Photographs. Virtually every local studies collection contains a wide range of old and contemporary photographs of the local community and, as often as not, of local personalities. The images held by local studies collections are often unique and, therefore, it makes perfect sense to include a good cross-section on the website. Additionally, it is important to remember that a website that has strong visual appeal is likely to stick in the minds of users. A lesson can easily be learned here from the experiences at Knowsley where a strong standardised house style with a black background was adopted. This has proved to be particularly effective for showing off black and white photographs.

A website is also a useful mechanism whereby the authority can appeal for additional photographs. The site should include a list of subjects that the library is particularly anxious to obtain images for as the web offers the potential to extend such appeals far beyond the reaches of the conventional local press.

Photographs should be arranged and presented in an imaginative way. All too often images are simply incorporated into sites as a means of enlivening text rather than real thought being given to the importance of the image itself.

Knowsley is not alone in adopting a more interactive approach (reflecting each of the communities within the borough). Manchester City Council Libraries have created a Local Image Collection and have adopted a commendably interactive approach with their 'Picture your street' which encourages users to nominate places to be included on the site:

> Your chance to tell us why a particular Manchester street means a lot to you and persuade us to publish a historical picture of it on this website.[5]

Ideally, as happens with Manchester's collection, there should be a mechanism whereby the entire collection of online images can be searched using keyword searching. Additionally, the appeal of old photographs in commercial terms should not be forgotten and consideration should be given to including an e-business option enabling users, particularly remote ones, to purchase copies of photographs of interest. Many local studies departments offer this service to face-to-face users for images that they possess the copyright of and realistically this can and should be extended to remote users as well.

Q is for Quality. The quality of the website is of paramount importance. Users appreciate both quality and quantity and many feel that they know a website that they can 'trust' intuitively. While their methods for reaching this conclusion may well be entirely subjective and not based on the criteria generally applied by information professionals, librarians should not underestimate their ability to identify a good quality site when they see one. The collection will possess a wide range of materials, many of them authoritative and the product of serious scholarly research over many years. These need to be drawn on in order to provide text of a high quality. The graphics used and particularly the quality of image reproductions on the website are of great importance. The best quality photographs should be scanned for inclusion on the site. Quality should not be sacrificed in order to provide a quick fix. To a certain extent the Internet has made information professionals of all who use it. The lay person is often better at making value judgements about quality than the librarian is perhaps willing to give them credit for.

R is for Research. Research is a two-way process and the website must encourage this. On the one hand, the website exists to foster research at all levels and encourage all users to persevere with their studies. However, equally importantly, the website should encourage users to consider how their own research may be disseminated for the greater good of the community and for the assistance of other users and researchers that come after.

A useful mechanism (one more generally adopted in local history websites in the United States) is to encourage the publishing of individual (or group) projects on the Internet. In the United States, the Folkways and Valley of the Shadow websites have both deliberately sought to include individuals' outputs on their sites from schoolchildren's projects to postgraduate research and everything in between. The inclusion of a 'what our users have done' or 'recent research section' may be a valuable mechanism for achieving this. Consequently, if space permits, local studies websites may be used to mount some users' investigations in exactly the same way as they might have previously sold copies of local studies books.

S is for Searching. The site should be capable of supporting keyword searching, enabling users to find references to the themes they are interested in even if the site is arranged by chronology or by location. Searching facilities should be as intuitive as the software used will allow. Similarly, the navigation of the site should be as logical and user-friendly as possible. Ideally, the website should be piloted on independent testers before it is launched. A site map should certainly be included showing what each section contains.

T is for Thumbnail. The visual appeal of the site needs to be balanced against the practical issues associated with access. The inclusion of lots of images is undoubtedly a good thing but users with limited IT facilities should be borne in mind when creating the site. It is important to remember that many remote users may be using dial-up modem connections with limited speed and the downloading of pages with large image content may impede their access. Lengthy downloads, like broken hyperlinks, discourage users and result in them being unlikely to explore the site as fully as might be hoped. Consequently, if a page has a large number of images included on it, consideration should be given to the use of thumbnails which leaves the user in control of deciding exactly which images they wish to see full-size.

U is for Utility. It is important not to overlook the utilitarian aspects of the site in a headlong rush for interactivity. A good site will tie in the e-content with the physical collection. It will explain clearly what resources are held and how they relate to one another. It will provide finding aids and, quite possibly, 'how to...' guides to get the unfamiliar started. Balance is again important in this context. Sites which are purely utilitarian and describe the collection and nothing else do indeed tend to be dull.

However, there is an equal danger in making a site too sophisticated and not making that all-important connection with the actual collection itself. The website, no matter how sophisticated, should whet the appetites of users and encourage them into the collection wherever possible. The basic information about the collection needs to be included alongside the mundane details such as location, mailing address, telephone number and opening times. The utilitarian aspects should not be sacrificed in favour of the dramatic.

V is for Visual. The visual appeal of the website should be of paramount concern. Unfortunately, it is often the case that sites with excellent content are let down by scant attention having been paid to the aesthetics of the site. Conversely, some visually appealing sites are often degraded by poor quality content. It is essential to get the balance right. It is likely that web design experts (perhaps from the parent organisation) will be heavily involved in this part of the project. The creation of a house style for the site is essential and the aesthetic appeal requires to be considered. Garish colours should be avoided and standard fonts and font sizes should be adopted.

W is for Wording. The text should be accessible and easily understandable to a wide range of users. At the planning stage it is important to remember the huge diversity of people likely to access the website from young children to senior citizens, those with extensive knowledge of the community and those with none. Equally importantly, the text should be accurate and derived from authoritative sources. The text should be scholarly and accessible. Very careful consideration should be given to the choice of font, the size, the colour, the positioning on the page and what constitutes an 'adequate' length of paragraph, and those with expertise in web design should certainly be involved in this aspect (as mentioned above). The site should not shy away from the inclusion of local dialect as this invariably adds an interesting flavour to any local website but all such uses of the vernacular should be clearly explained. The ethnic mix of the community is important. Parallel pages in minority languages should be considered. The collective memory of the community is not simply about those people who have always been there but it is also about new communities.

X is for Xenial. The entire website must be user-friendly and hospitable, created very definitely with the user in mind. The website will be representative of the library as a whole and of the local studies department in particular and, consequently, the site must reflect a welcoming ethos for all users and potential users. The user-friendliness is, to a certain extent, a marriage of all the other aspects in this A to Z but it is an important feature to be considered from the very outset. Particularly important are issues surrounding the language and tone, the format, the style and, of course, subject matter. However, it is also related to the mechanics of web design as well. The layout must be logical and easily navigated, the links must work, and the promises that the site makes must be demonstrably capable of being fulfilled.

A user-friendly site is one that is regularly maintained and updated (without embarking on frequent and wholesale reconstructions that do not serve any particular purpose). Users like new, additional features but they also value continuity; they do not like sites being redesigned for the sake of it, making once familiar navigation paths more difficult. If maintenance has to be undertaken or changes made then users should be notified. The inclusion of a 'What's New' or even 'Site Status' section is helpful, particularly so if the construction is an ongoing process. It is better to flag up early (near the homepage if at all possible) that certain sections are either under construction or subject to revision. This is a better approach than allowing users to burrow down into the site only to come up against an array of 'under construction messages'. At the end of the day, the site is for the benefit of users, not the library.

Y is for Yell. Perhaps a somewhat tongue-in-cheek penultimate entry for an A to Z but yell means shout and shouting draws attention and that is something which local studies websites desperately require. The onus must be on the librarian to yell about the site and to promote it and publicise it as much as possible. All too often local studies sites are buried in the depths of the library services pages, difficult to find and difficult to navigate. This is often exacerbated in both the public and academic sectors because the library's pages themselves can often be hidden within the general website of the organisation itself. The library might often be proud of them but no one else is because no one else has really noticed that they exist.

The site (or indeed major revisions or updates to the site) should be launched in a 'blaze of publicity'. In many cases local studies department have good links with the local media and this is the time to call in favours. Posters and leaflets should be produced and circulated to local organisations. The creators need to ensure that it is picked up by the major search engines and other local sites need to be encouraged to put in hyperlinks.

The publicising of the site is often hindered by long and complicated universal resource locators (URLs) because the site is a directory of a directory. The librarian should try to encourage the ICT specialists to provide as concise and as mnemonic a URL as possible. Consideration should even be given to purchasing a unique domain name. The parent organisation's server can still host the site but a unique and easily memorised URL (such as *http://history.knowsley .gov.uk*) has huge advantages. Completely independent URLs may be eschewed for political reasons but these can be purchased relatively inexpensively and can help increase traffic on the site.

Z is for Zip. The ability to zip or compress files for inclusion on the Internet is important as we have seen from the mention of thumbnail images earlier. This enables the inclusion of larger files that might otherwise be disregarded as too big or taking too long to download. Many software packages (such as WinZip) are widely available and widely used and many have free versions available for downloading. Although not an absolutely essential point, it is worth considering whether zipped material can be included.

Conclusion

Local studies departments can learn a great deal from the electronic initiatives that have been undertaken in other parts of the library, most notably in terms of the provision that is available within the reference department itself. Much has been written about the provision of digital, virtual or electronic reference services and much of this is transferable into the local studies context. Of course, the local studies department must provide access to the enquiry-answering sources in the shape of the national or international tools that are available such as Family Search or the Census online. However, the great benefit of local studies collections lies almost entirely in the *local* dimension. It is perhaps arguable that while endless lists and headings for content creation can be suggested, the ultimate strength of a local studies collection's website lies exclusively in the local material that is included. Much can be learned from the examples of good practice that currently exist and Knowsley remains pre-eminent among these. A local studies website must be responsive to users and to the local community. Its content must reflect both of these. Local studies collections are cultural entities that celebrate diversity. This is surely their strength in reality – and so too must it be their strength virtually as well.

Notes

1. Peter Marchant and Eileen Hume (1998) 'Visiting Knowsley's past', *Library Association Record*, 100(9): 468–9.
2. Marchant and Hume, 'Visting Knowsley's past'.

3. *Folkways – Putting Local Knowledge Online*, available at *http://www .folkways.org/*.

4. C. Cochrane (1985) 'Public libraries and the changing nature of oral history', *Audiovisual Librarian*, 11(4): 201–7.

5. 'Picture Your Street', Manchester City Libraries; available at *http://www.manchester.gov.uk/libraries/* (accessed May 2003).

5

E-genealogy and the library

Introduction

If local history was once regarded as an inferior branch of history then family history was once dismissed as little more than an entertaining sideline with some librarians regarding 'the family tree people' as little more than a nuisance. This is a position which is no longer tenable for librarians and, in the digital age, such a view has become positively naive. Genealogy is frequently cited in surveys of the top-ten uses of the Internet[1] and, as a hobby, it has increased in popularity dramatically over the last twenty years. The advent of e-genealogy has meant a further explosion in interest and requires local studies libraries to be proactive and take practical steps to provide a high quality of service.

This chapter addresses the ways in which libraries can do this and particularly emphasises that web-based provision – often in the shape of gateways – needs to be a dynamic mixture of national and international sources with local and area-specific ones. Such a gateway can be created in a relatively inexpensive fashion while still providing a valued-added service. The argument may be advanced that, in itself, a gateway does not necessarily increase accessibility to a library's own collection because most of the sites linked to it would be external ones.

However, this perhaps means that libraries need to address the issue of their own digital archive more actively. Electronic provision can also facilitate the provision of outreach genealogical services within the community itself because genealogical services may still be largely concentrated in one library in any (public) authority's area. An e-genealogy gateway consolidates these remote services in a 'one-stop site' and results in branch libraries which hitherto may not have had much in the way of family history resources being able to, with the aid of an Internet connection, provide some degree of access to sources and services.

It also examines the materials which should be included and the sites which should be linked to as well as discussing some of the pitfalls and dangers of an over-reliance on electronic genealogical sources. In this field, more than almost any other associated with local studies, it is vital to remember the importance, perhaps even the pre-eminent importance, of the original, hard-copy sources. The benefits of creating digital local resources has been mentioned in Chapter 4 but this emphasised the role that the library itself has in the creation and dissemination of electronic resources about the local area. This is less easy with genealogy but is more than compensated for by the vast array of materials already in existence from other information providers.

Building an e-genealogy gateway

The compilation of local history gateways in libraries is still in its infancy. A particularly commendable site is the

Toronto-based 'Historicity' (*http://historicity.tpl.toronto.on.ca/*). In Wales, the 'Gathering the Jewels' website (*http://www.gtj.org.uk/gtj/*) aims to collect together some of the most outstanding artefacts, documents, photographs and the like from libraries and archives throughout the country. Many main reference departments may well have done this in connection with contemporary living, creating gateways or, at least, bookmarking local information sites in connection with health, welfare, education, employment, public administration and so on, but similarly thorough efforts exclusively for local history are perhaps less common. Very often, even the best local studies websites end up with a series of links to other sites and give the appearance of having been compiled without much thought. Given that family and community history are so inextricably linked it is necessary to take a more thorough approach.

Good e-genealogy provision recognises the essential mix of national and local sources. The State Library of Queensland has developed a particularly useful guide to genealogy and the Internet which provides fifty pages of detailed advice on using the Internet for family history (*http://www.slq.qld.gov.au/scd/famhist/*). The Queensland service successfully combines advice and guidance with tutorials and activities both at the local and the international level, recognising that many in their community will wish to trace their lineage back to Europe. Seattle Public Library has also developed a useful site although it relies more heavily on core national and international sources (and commercial ones at that) rather than local ones (*http://www.spl.org/selectedsites/genealogy.html*).

As Chapter 2 outlined, parochialism has gone global and the Internet encourages this trend. Genealogical research tends to emphasise this because many people researching their family history in North America or Australia and New Zealand ultimately succeed in tracing their ancestry back to Europe. This globalisation of sources is particularly noticeable in terms of e-genealogy. Whether it is using an indexing site like Family Search or a discussion forum like RootsWeb it is perfectly possible for an Australian sitting in the comfort of their own home to access data about their ancestry in Orkney. However, there does exist a distinction here. It is perfectly possible to access raw data; finding value-added information on family history using the Web is often more problematic.

The challenge for library managers in general and innovative local studies librarians in particular is to see how these global sources can be usefully related to the local ones. It is important that gateways created by local studies departments include both the global sources and also, and perhaps more importantly, informs users about local sources and services available to them. Terrick FitzHugh describes genealogy as

> biographical research into one's forebears with the object of compiling a narrative history of the family. A family history should place members of the family in their historical, geographical, social and occupational contexts and describe their activities and the lives they lived.[2]

Very often e-genealogy sites are exceptionally good at providing the raw data and are capable of placing members of the family in their basic historical and geographical contexts. But the electronic sources are often very weak at providing the social and occupational contexts and do not provide the much-sought-after details of how they lived their lives. This is where the librarian, on a very local level, can step in.

So what can the local studies department offer in the way of e-genealogical provision when many of the sources are at a national level? The answer really lies in the interpretation of the word 'genealogy' and here it is necessary to look back at FitzHugh's definition and to stress that virtually all aspects of local and community history can fulfil a role within family history.

Genealogical gateways do already exist on the Internet and provide one-stop shops for the major tools, the online indices, the national and international sources, the discussion threads and bulletin boards. The site Cyndi's List (*http://www.cyndislist.com/*) provides links to over 180,000 genealogical web pages from around the globe. However, such gateways as currently exist tend not be area specific; they tend not to merge together what FitzHugh's definition would seem to suggest is essential – the materials that provide the background and context with those that provide the raw data.

Within the United Kingdom and Ireland one of the most effective sites is Genuki (Genealogy United Kingdom and

Ireland) (see Figure 5.1). Genuki contains a wealth of information and links and provides both national and very local details, county by county and parish by parish. Additionally, Genuki provides brief descriptions of individual parishes taken from historical gazetteers.

Figure 5.1 The homepage of Genuki

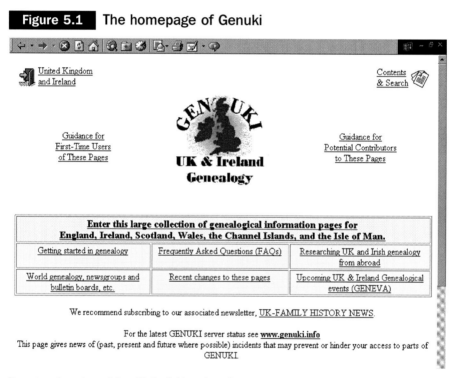

Reproduced courtesy of Genuki. Available at *http://www.genuki.org.uk/*.

Before examining the provision of local materials for genealogy it is necessary to examine some of the broad categories of generic materials and the electronic sources available to access them.

Parish registers and their indices

Old Parish Registers (OPRs) of births, marriages and deaths are, of course, one of the principal sources available for the genealogist and they are widely available in microfilmed format in many local studies departments. Generally speaking, few local studies collections have original parish registers, which tend to remain the property of the churches concerned and in any case are too fragile to stand up to the constant and heavy use they would receive. Consequently, record offices, archives or, in some cases, the churches themselves have microfilmed the vast majority of registers. These contain baptismal, marriage and funeral entries. The details can vary from parish to parish and from religious denomination to denomination. This is often one of the biggest problems for family historians as well as local studies librarians: certain registers may not be available for particular faiths, the quality of the information can vary dramatically (frequently explained away by apocryphal stories of the drunken clergyman in the 1780s who never bothered to update his living's registers).

Digitised copies of OPRs are relatively uncommon and it would be hugely costly to undertake this on any meaningful level. Consequently, it tends to be indices rather than the registers themselves which become the focus of electronic provision of the information contained in OPRs. The contents of parish registers for the Docklands area of London is, however, available on ParishRegister.com (see Figure 5.2).

Figure 5.2 Parish Register

Reproduced courtesy of Mr James Legon. Available at *http://www.parishregister.com/*.

Family Search: the electronic IGI

The main indexing tool for OPRs is the International Genealogical Index (IGI), produced by the Church of Jesus Christ of the Latter-day Saints (the Mormons). IGI has indices to over 90 per cent of births and marriages in Old Parish Registers. The figure is significantly less for deaths because of the infrequency with which necrologies were kept in many parishes. Many local studies libraries have long held IGI in microfiche format and this has been a mainstay of genealogical provision. The most frequently used microfiche version of IGI has been that arranged by county and then alphabetically by surname (although there is also an additional version arranged by country then alphabetically by surname so it is possible to search all of Wales or Sweden or whatever country the user is interested in). Both of these versions enable the user (or indeed the librarian) to gain easy access to the materials held in the parish registers themselves. The references gained here allow the user to pinpoint the exact date of birth, marriage or death and therefore to access easily the actual entry in the OPR. It is important, however, not to forget the original Old Parish Registers in all of this. IGI does indeed contain the names of spouses or parents but the original registers may contain other valuable information such as the names of witnesses, sponsors or godparents at a particular event or some vital piece of information may be gleaned from another entry on the same page that is picked up purely by chance.

In recent years it has been complemented by the arrival of the Family Search (*http://www.familysearch.org/*) website. This has revolutionised the genealogist's access to one of the most useful sources. Family Search means that genealogists who once relied on visiting the library to consult the microfiche versions of IGI can now sit at home and retrieve information, free of charge, from the index over the Internet from anywhere in the world. It is probably not understating the case by saying that Family Search has, very rapidly, become the most important single genealogy site on the Internet.

The Family Search website, while undoubtedly a tremendous resource, has one disadvantage over the microfiche version and it is one which should not be underestimated either by the library professional or by the genealogist – that is the ability to browse or, at least, the ability to browse *all* the entries for a particular name. The website's information retrieval system makes both first name and surname required fields for searching and therefore makes it impossible to generate a list of all people with a particular surname. The user interface specifies required fields and these are always first name and surname. Here the microfiche has a decided advantage, particularly if it is an unusual surname that is being investigated and where the assumption might be that all people bearing that surname in a certain locality may be related to one another. For example, it would be beneficial for a researcher investigating the Sudding family to be able to retrieve a full list of everyone with that surname (given that the family is of German extraction and that the name is very uncommon in the United Kingdom).

The reasoning behind this is obvious when it comes to very common names and Family Search would indeed buckle under the pressure of a search for everyone named Smith in England or everyone named Schmidt in Germany. Consequently, it would also be useful to have, on the web version, a mechanism whereby searches can be limited by place (which is possible in microfiche by using the version arranged by county or district). Family Search does facilitate the limiting of searches in the USA (by state, which is still a relatively blunt tool given that many of the states have populations larger than entire European countries) but limiting by county or province is not a supported search technique for other countries. It is possible to search Family

Search using a more sophisticated interface which will support specific place searching through some of the subscription websites but the free-at-the-point-of-use site does not offer this facility.

The International Genealogical Index and the Old Parish Registers do share common problems. Both are lacking in consistency in terms of nomenclature and in terms of the level of detail provided and this may often cause headaches to researchers. For example, Jeans often become Janes or Williams may be entered as Wm. IGI has transcribed precisely the parish records themselves so if William is entered as 'Wm' in the actual record IGI simply replicates it. This has always been a slight problem with the fiche version but Family Search's retrieval mechanism is sophisticated enough to overcome this and will retrieve Williams and Wms together (although it will also support searching for a specific spelling by a simple 'tick box' option on the search interface). In one respect the lack of specificity in terms of geographical searching can also have a beneficial affect. In some cases, children may have been baptised twice in different parishes (if, for example, the mother and father of the child came, themselves, from different parishes). Family Search picks this up with no problem at all.

The omission of 10 per cent of birth and marriage registers in IGI (and thus also omitted from Family Search) can be significant. Many of the smaller denominations or sects may not appear in IGI for a variety of reasons (including the loss of the original records or because the denomination chose not to become involved in the Mormons' project). A number of local studies departments or family history societies have indexed additional registers, copies of which they may have in their possession. However, electronic dissemination of these is relatively uncommon. Local studies websites should, however, make a concerted effort to alert users to the existence of these sources, particularly through their websites. This may lead to a concomitant increase in enquiries (especially from remote users) but these sources are often of tremendous importance in family history research.

In some cases, however, the indices and, indeed, the registers themselves do not necessarily tell the whole story. Just because someone was baptised or married in the Established Churches (in the United Kingdom, the Church of England or the Church of Scotland) does not necessarily mean they were adherents of that faith. The parties may have married in that church for the sake of legal convenience if their own faith was persecuted. This is most significant with marriages where, historically, the legal requirement was to marry in the Established Church, even though both parties in matrimony may have been members of dissenting congregations.

This notion of the sources presenting only partial evidence is significant in all aspects of family history. One of the dangers associated with electronic indices is that, viewed in isolation and without access to the original registers (or at the very least surrogates for them), an over-reliance is placed on the index alone and that information is not properly cross-referenced. It is important to bear in mind that sources such as IGI, whether microfiche or electronic, are ultimately *only* indexing tools and that the full and meaningful primary data is only available in the actual Old Parish Registers themselves.

This is perhaps more of an issue with Family Search than with IGI on fiche because of the remote access it provides. In some ways, this remote access is both its greatest strength and also, perhaps, one of its biggest weaknesses. Clearly, the remote access that Family Search provides renders huge benefits to researchers globally but they must be careful not to accept unquestioningly the index entry just because they cannot easily access the OPR remotely.

Equally, for local studies libraries, the ease with which individuals can retrieve information from a tool such as Family Search inevitably leads to great demands being put on the library services. Those users that recognise that IGI/Family Search is *only* an indexing tool will inevitably want material from the primary sources (the OPRs) and may well inundate libraries with requests for copies from microfilmed parish registers. The Internet has made this easier but the consequence in terms of staff time and resources within local studies departments have not been fully assessed.

Joined-up thinking

The development of the Origins.net websites (which cover England, Scotland and Ireland) have been the first attempt at 'joined-up thinking' for accessing genealogical resources. Origins.net provides exclusive access to the holdings of the Society of Genealogists and has hitherto been split into English Origins, Scots Origins and Irish Origins. Each of these take markedly different approaches with the materials they disseminate. English Origins does not, for example, provide access to statutory sources so it is not possible to access remotely registers of births, marriages and deaths (i.e. official birth, marriage and death certification). Irish Origins does not contain primary information itself but allows users free access to some 24,000 web pages among which can be found census data, church records and valuation rolls.

Perhaps the most interesting and important development of Origins.net has been the replacement of the Scots Origins service with Scotland's People (*http://www.scotlandspeople.gov.uk/*) on 1 September 2002 (see Figure 5.3). This is now the definitive electronic genealogy service provided by the General Register Office for Scotland and can be fairly said to be one of the most significant and, indeed, comprehensive electronic genealogy initiatives on the Web. Scotland's People is one of the most impressive electronic genealogy sites available because it brings together in one place all of the principal sources.

Through it the user can search OPRs, census returns and the statutory registers of births, marriages and deaths. Additionally, one of the problems about Family Search outlined earlier, namely that it cannot be searched by discrete geographical area, has been overcome on the Scotland's People website which provides an improved interface for searching the IGI and supports direct searching by parish. Inevitably, however, the site is not free at the point of use and requires the purchasing of credits to carry out searches. Additional payment is required if a copy of an item is required.

Figure 5.3 Scotland's People

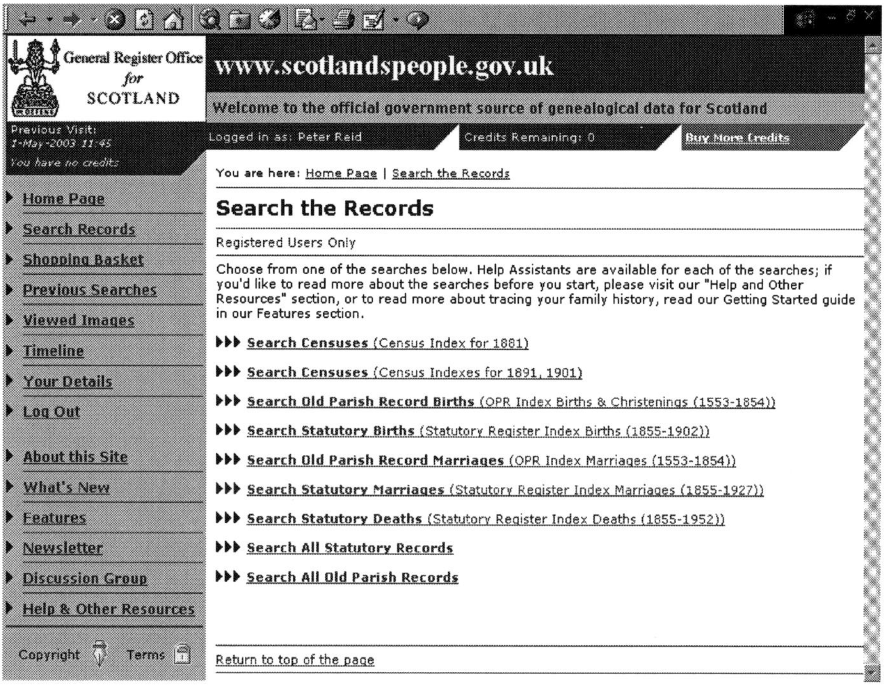

Reproduced courtesy of the General Register Office for Scotland. Available at
http://www.scotlandspeople.gov.uk/.

For a fee, it is possible to search the index and then order a copy of the certificate required (but being able to identify the certificate requires a high level of information beforehand). A charge is made for obtaining the copy which is then delivered through the post. This is undoubtedly of significant advantage to remote searchers who are not within easy travelling distance of the appropriate registry office or country records office. Scotland's People is an important advance in e-genealogical provision.

Censuses

When many people think of family history they automatically think of census returns. Census data provides more detail than the simple mechanics of a baptism or a marriage. Many amateur genealogists, often encouraged by local studies librarians who know only too well the difficulties of tracing families back through the generations, are now keen to find out as much as they can about their ancestors and what life was like for them. They are no longer simply content to find out endless lists of names and dates vanishing backwards into the mists of time.

Census returns provide the first step in finding out more about the individuals because the returns provide addresses, occupations, the place where individuals were born and, of course, in one fell swoop details about offspring and other family members dwelling in the household. At first, some of the details appear unimpressive to the uninitiated, such as how many rooms the household occupied, but these small, individual details supply indicators to the prosperity or otherwise of the family and collectively enable a much more broadly-based picture of family history to be developed.

Census records have, for some time, been available on CD-Rom and this has proved to be a popular alternative for libraries to microfilmed versions. However, increasingly the CD-Roms are coming to be seen as yesterday's technology and, more recently, there has been a move towards online provision of the census materials. It is perhaps due to this increased desire to know more about individuals and their lives that has lead to the phenomenal popularity of sites offering access to census materials online. So popular was electronic access to the 1901 Census on the Public Record Office's website (now part of the National Archives) that the system ground to a halt.

The levels of interest in the online census demonstrate admirably that family history has ceased to be simply about a vague list of names and dates and has become more encompassing. In many cases, amateur genealogists and library users want to find out much more about their ancestors than when they were born and when they died. Old Parish Records might provide the skeletal frame and census returns might add a little flesh to the bones but it is the plethora of other, often obscure, sources in local studies departments that provide an insight into the souls of ancestors.

This is the challenge for local studies departments and their librarians. The increased interest in genealogical investigation is accompanied by an increased interest in community history too. Users of local studies departments want to know much more about their ancestors than just the bare facts. Librarians often quite rightly encourage this because the number of sources available covering aspects of life in the nineteenth century is vast in comparison to earlier periods. It is often easier, therefore, to provide a more detailed picture of the lives of ancestors in the nineteenth century than it is to progress a genealogy back beyond the eighteenth century. The arrival of services such as Origins.net has reinforced the need for local studies libraries to look again at their own materials and their own delivery of genealogical services. With national information providers leading the way in the provision of the raw materials of family history – the registers, the censuses and the like – it falls to local studies departments to provide the background and context that many family historians crave.

What's missing?

A great many valuable genealogical resources remain largely inaccessible electronically. One of the most significant is the vast body of information that is available on monumental inscriptions (MIs) in graveyards. By and large, published monumental inscriptions have been transcribed by teams of volunteers working under the auspices of the various local family history societies. The information is inevitably very partial because only a minority of people could afford monumental headstones with inscriptions.

Often these are compiled into small volumes which are sold by the societies. For many family history societies these publications provide a steady, if modest, source of income and there is, therefore, an understandable reluctance to provide free Internet access to them. Providing a pay-per-view system for these indices on family history society websites is very often not an option as these sites are often not sophisticated enough to support secure electronic payment and, in many cases, as these volumes are inexpensive, librarians and users prefer to possess the hard-copy versions. One very useful electronic source is the National Burial Register which, although partial, provides invaluable data.

Many local studies departments hold valuation rolls for properties within their area. These are very useful sources for the family historian, especially once the basic details have been identified from the censuses. These again add value to family history by providing information on tenants, rateable values and landlords. Many will have originally been produced by county councils or local authorities and will have been deposited either in local studies departments or county archives for convenient storage. Similarly, school rolls may have been deposited in the same fashion. The local studies librarians could give consideration to making some of these available remotely. One local heritage group did include digitised copies of a local valuation role on their website (although it lacked any searching technique and users would simply have to come across relevant entries by chance) (see Figure 5.4).

| Figure 5.4 | Port Gordon Valuation Rolls |

Reproduced courtesy of Port Gordon Local History Online. Available at *http://www.portgordon.org/*.

Photographs perhaps offer one of the biggest opportunities and are an area particularly suited to delivery over the Internet. Most local studies departments have extensive collections of both old and contemporary photographs; these have often been successfully exploited in the past through hard-copy 'past and present' type publications because the copyright of many of the images rests with the local authority and, therefore, presents no problems in terms of reproduction. Exactly the same can be done over the Internet as a number of innovative local studies departments have shown. Manchester, in particular, has sought to exploit its photographic collections in the 'Picture your street' section of its website (as mentioned earlier in Chapters 1 and 4).

Indeed this site positively encourages an interactive response both from local people and those further afield by asking for suggestions for other images to be incorporated into the site. To date, however, the widespread exploitation of photographic collections remains somewhat disappointing.

Many local studies departments have created local studies indices which may, in many cases, be focused towards facilitating access to the wealth of information contained in old local newspapers. A few of these indices remain in hard copy but increasingly they are electronic. However, in most cases these indices remain retrieval tools within the physical confines of the library and have not been made available remotely using the Internet. Local newspapers are important sources of genealogical information and not simply in terms of birth and death notices. In many cases, newspaper reports may enable the genealogist to find out the background to people and places. Increasingly, on a more general level, libraries see it as appropriate to make their online public access catalogues available through the Web, essentially for the benefit of local users. Taking this one step further it would seem sensible to also make available local studies indices through the Internet.

Discussion threads

Family history discussion threads have emerged as one of the most beneficial tools of e-genealogy for they enable researchers working on the same name or in the same geographic vicinity to come together, exchange information and post questions or queries. Sites such as Genealogy.com with its GenForum for individual surnames or RootsWeb.com with its fora for particular counties or geographical areas both provide interactivity and communication that was difficult before the advent of the Internet. Many family history societies have recognised the importance of the interactivity of these threads and have sought to facilitate easier communication between their members by including, in addition to postal addresses of members, their e-mail address too. Hitherto, contacts with others researching in the same field often depended largely on serendipity.

However, the benefits come at a price and one that is particularly significant for libraries which pride themselves on providing access to reliable, quality information. The one major problem that often emerges strongly from such discussion threads – and, indeed, seems to bedevil genealogy in general and e-genealogy in particular – is that of jumping to conclusions. The good genealogist knows – in the same way as the professional information worker knows – that assumptions should not be made on partial evidence, but this is a temptation which many amateur genealogists find difficult to resist. Undertaking family history remotely, relying almost exclusively on electronic sources and services, seems to lead many amateurs into making unsustainable assumptions based on very partial evidence, most frequently that the name and the date *seem* right so therefore must *be* right. Very often this practice is most noticeable from those doing their researches at greatest distance and underlying these assumptions is often a not-so-touchingly naive lack of comprehension about the 'the old country'.

Consequently, family history discussion threads often contain messages and information or comments of dubious reliability. They often include messages from one side of the world claiming that the researcher has traced his or her lineage back to 1087, when it is all too evident to librarians and researchers on the other side of the world that the existing records do not go further back than 1620. Or that the researcher's family (the Greens) comes from Devon so are 'related to all the West Country Greens'.

So what, if anything, can librarians be doing about this? The simple answer is nothing. Unless a gateway is intended to provide links to quality-checked sites (and that in itself is problematic and tend to move gateways away from being simple, inexpensive solutions) then the best that the librarian can do is put a disclaimer on the reliability, quality and authoritativeness of external sites. Ideally, this should be done as a pop-up message as soon as a hyperlink from the gateway is clicked-on.

Conclusion

Librarians would not conceive of leaving hard-copy material uncatalogued, unclassified and unsorted. So why should it be any different for digital resources? Indeed the case for logically arranging local material on the Internet is, if anything, stronger for web-based material because it can be accessed globally and because there is so much material out there. It is a rather simplistic solution to suggest that anyone capable of using a search engine can easily access local materials. It is in the library's interests to have a front-end which includes a gateway to as many local sites as possible. Librarians, who already have sophisticated information-gathering skills, will, in many cases, have bookmarked the majority of these sites anyway and it makes perfect sense to move beyond bookmarking to share easy access with those who may not necessarily possess the same level of information retrieval skills as librarians. Obviously, there are issues associated with staff time and resources to achieve this but a haphazard approach to local electronic sites is no longer really appropriate.

Various attempts have been made to set up local 'legal' deposit schemes whereby all publications produced locally or about local subject matters are deposited in local studies departments (not, however, like the national Legal Deposit which ensures the free provisions of texts). Allied to this needs to be a systematic strategy for identifying as comprehensive a list as possible of local history websites relating to the area. Many of these websites will have been put together by local organisations or by private individuals. These sites might relate to a particular town, village or parish; they might be related to a particular industry or trade or they might relate to a particular subject. Additionally, many other local websites may also have a historical component and these are worthy of examination and inclusion.

The next chapter fully explores the importance of collaboration and cooperation between local studies departments and other external agencies and organisations. However, it is important to examine cooperation in the context of providing valuable background information for the genealogist. This is not simply a case of building up a tolerably good relationship with the local family history society or the registrar or the archives. Rather it is about enabling e-genealogists to give context to their endeavours both through accessing library materials remotely but also by easily and efficiently enabling face-to-face patrons to find additional information by accessing other sites. E-genealogy has proved to be one of the enduring success stories of the Internet and given its central role within local studies collections, it is important that libraries fully embrace web-based technologies as part of their service delivery in this area.

Notes

1. Some surveys show genealogy second only to sex as the most popular use of the Internet.
2. Terrick FitzHugh (1998) *Dictionary of Genealogy*, 5th edn. London: A & C Black.

6

E-collaboration and cooperation

Introduction

No local studies department can be said to have complete coverage for its area. Indeed no library, however comprehensive it aims to be, can truly boast this. Collaboration and cooperation with external agencies and organisations should be a central feature of local studies work. In conventional terms this works on a number of levels, for example fostering links with schools to identify the needs of students or developing good relations with local societies which may have materials that would be beneficial to the collection. However, e-collaboration suggests something more. On the one hand, it may be examined in terms of involvement in consortia to create electronic resources (for example, the digitisation of a photographic collection) but on the other it can be taken to mean expanding the service beyond the confines of the collection within the department itself to bring in sources and services from remote locations. This chapter presents a practical guide to web-based collaboration and cooperation between local studies libraries and their staff with external organisations, both local and further afield, and will demonstrate the practical benefits to library services of fostering such relationships.

Providers of local studies materials

One of the most important things for anyone involved in local studies to remember, whether they be a practitioner or a user, is that the local studies library is only one of a sometimes bewildering array of providers of local materials. However, in most cases the first and most obvious provider will be the main local studies department, as often as not located in or near the principal or central library. This centralised approach is not without its benefits but, in some cases, the centralisation of a local studies collection in one location can cause problems and even resentment. This is often particularly true of rural areas where there is sometimes a perception that the largest town gets all the benefits while smaller communities are sometimes neglected. Conscious of this, a number of public authorities have deliberately sought to provide reasonably-sized collections in branch libraries. Some authorities, mindful of loyalties to a particular district that may no longer exist in political or geographic terms, have deliberately chosen to maintain collections in a variety of locations throughout their area. Local government reorganisation has led to some collections which were previously subsumed into larger, perhaps county-wide collections re-emerging as unitary and discrete collections.

However, the public library sector is by no means the only provider of local studies materials, with academic libraries often maintaining collections not to mention the private collections of local organisations and societies. Michael Dewe in his chapter on resource providers in *Local Studies Collection Management* (2002) provides an excellent overview of the very diverse range of bodies involved in the provision of local materials.

Collaborative analysis

In the past, filling gaps or partial coverage in a local studies collection was largely viewed in terms of conventional stock acquisition policies (however unconventional the mechanisms might be to acquire local materials). However, the Internet challenges local studies librarians to look at this in a new and more dynamic manner. It is now possible to offer remote access to materials held elsewhere but of interest to the local community in association with other collections and organisations both locally and nationally and, in some cases, internationally. Imagination and ambition can make the seemingly impossible possible. Dunfermline Public Library – proud of its links with Andrew Carnegie on a local level – can now, with the aid of the Internet, link to rich sources of information about him in the United States, sources which, to the ordinary person on the Dunfermline omnibus, might have once remained a closed mystery. And those in the United States can get access to the library in Scotland.

Before serious e-collaboration and cooperation can be undertaken it is essential that there is some degree of basic analysis of the contents of the collection. This should focus on all aspects but it is particularly important to identify the gaps or areas in which there is a varying degree of partial coverage. In many cases, staff will already be all-too-familiar with the gaps and will probably know exactly where complementary materials are held – it may be the local archives, it may be a local historical society or it may be a university library. Indeed, in many cases, a procedure may be in place for providing referral to these services. However, there may well be instances where no complementary collection has been identified and the resources of the local studies library are very much confined to those within its four walls. Yet it is very seldom the case that there is nothing supplementary or related elsewhere even with apparently 'unique' holdings.

However, e-collaboration is not simply about remote collection. It is equally important to consider this in terms of active involvement with other local organisations and bodies. One mechanism available is through the use of 'virtual exhibitions' (either for their own sake or to accompany and complement a 'real' exhibition being staged at a local venue). Exhibitions have long offered an opportunity for the various bodies involved in local studies to come together for the benefit of the community. There are numerous examples each year of local studies libraries, archives and museums pulling together items to present exhibitions on a particular event or theme such as the Second World War or Victorian Life. Largely, however, these exhibitions have hitherto been presented with 'live' artefacts to 'real' users in the library, archive or museum. Such exhibitions are beneficial to all of the agencies involved and help to demonstrate a more 'joined-up' approach to the provision of local materials (sometimes a deceptively 'joined-up' approach that belies the real situation on the ground).

However, the Internet offers the potential to create virtual exhibitions which pull together materials from different locations without the artefact ever having to leave its home. Local studies departments can provide digital versions of photographs or newspaper reports and, in some cases, text on a particular topic; the archive may be able to provide digital versions of first-hand accounts of the events being covered while the museum may be able to provide images of artefacts associated with them. The more ambitious and sophisticated virtual exhibitions may also choose to include audio, video or virtual reality tours (the latter technique having been successfully used by a number of museums and stately homes on their websites). One of the most significant benefits of virtual exhibitions is that they can be archived and continue to be made accessible without too much difficulty for an indefinite period and, once created, the digital surrogates can be re-used and manipulated in different ways for the future.

One important feature of virtual exhibitions is to ensure that they are well publicised both through the Internet itself with, perhaps, banner advertisements on the organisation's homepage and through efficient and effective inclusion in search engines. Additionally, conventional advertising should be used including press releases and posters. Virtual exhibitions need to be made easily accessible and it is particularly important to obtain a short and mnemonic URL address. As URLs can be purchased at relatively cheap prices there should be no excuse for using a long, complicated multi-directory web address. If the parent organisation has some qualms about material going on a website with an address not associated with it then logos and links should be incorporated.

These need not be hugely complicated nor indeed highly technical projects. However, local studies librarians should investigate the potential of collaboration with external agencies that might be in a position to help with innovative technological approaches. Perhaps one of the best examples of this is the one mentioned extensively in Chapter 4 – Knowsley. Their website was a collaborative venture between Knowsley Libraries, Connect (part of Liverpool University's Computer Science Department), Lancashire Record Office and Prescot Museum. This has brought together three excellent sources of local information with those who have the technical skills to best exploit the materials. The result is not only an excellent site in terms of its content but also in terms of being a model of e-collaboration and cooperation. In more general terms, links between library schools and departments of computer science in the academic sphere on the one hand and public, academic and special libraries on the other should be fostered. Some library schools have already created very good and mutually beneficial links with their professional communities.

Locate and link

Collaboration must come in a variety of different forms. As well as the other materials that the librarians are aware of locally, they should be proactively searching for other related sources further afield. As has been mentioned earlier in this chapter, the onus must be on the librarian – as the information professional – to attempt to identify and locate allied materials in other collections. To this end, local studies librarians need to engage fully with the Internet as an information retrieval tool. They too need to become effective Internet searchers in the same way as most of their counterparts in the reference department have. Zumalt and Pasiczynyuk identified as early as 1998 that 61 per cent of reference enquiries could be dealt with using the Internet. Inevitably, local studies will always remain different but that difference is not a justification for playing down its usefulness as a tool. Effective Internet searching and information literacy must be as much core skills in the local studies librarian's armoury as it is in the reference librarian's and training within libraries obviously needs to reflect this. Indeed there is a case for Internet training specifically geared towards those working in local studies.

Consequently, it may be seen that the identification and analysis of the gaps in the collection is, therefore, only the first step. The second is to actively search the Web (and indeed other sources) for collections that are complementary. The librarian should be proactive in fostering relations with these other collections and external bodies and e-mail makes this a much less formal procedure. The chances are that they will be equally pleased to have details of complementary materials.

This can be achieved in a very inexpensive way with the judicious placing of a few hyperlinks in the websites of the respective organisations. However, it may well lead to deeper levels of e-collaboration. If the resources are significant enough there may well be a case for digitising them, thus making them accessible globally. In such circumstances, there may prove to be enough scope to apply jointly for funding to digitise the various parts of the collection. This is a fundamental goal of the People's Network and the New Opportunities Fund is particularly supportive of collaborative ventures for digital content creation. Indeed, consortia projects account for almost 80 per cent of all those funded through the New Opportunities Fund (to 20 per cent being undertaken as stand-alone projects). The idea of virtual exhibitions touched on earlier need not be limited to agencies and organisations within the immediate community. Similar exhibitions can just as easily be mounted by drawing together collections that are separated by great distances. Bringing together disparate collections on the same subject is surely one of the most positive aspects of the Internet.

Web-based activities for local studies are all too often summed up as being 'a useful marketing tool'. While the promotional benefits of an Internet presence are undeniable, the Internet offers opportunities and benefits far beyond marketing alone. Collaboration and cooperation with external bodies certainly heightens the profile of the collection but they also enable practical rewards as well. Expanding the resources is no longer simply about acquiring hard-copy materials; it is also about creative digital partnerships with others. This need not necessarily be all about digitisation of resources; often it can be about more simple and straightforward relationships, sometimes even just about reciprocal hyperlinks in websites.

The methodical trawling of the Internet does not, however, make for a complete strategy. Various techniques need to be put in place to ensure that cooperation is meaningful and seen to be meaningful in the electronic environment. Many local studies departments (or at least the main reference department) will maintain fairly accurate and comprehensive lists of local organisations and their contacts. The updating of this information should always ask for a web address and e-mail contacts. This information needs to be shared between reference and local studies staff. Additionally, a lesson can be learned from the major Internet search engines which all provide options for the creators of websites to submit their sites for inclusion in the engine. A similar mechanism should be incorporated onto local studies websites. This need not be a complex or particularly costly mechanism. An online submission form, not too dissimilar from online enquiry submission forms, can be uploaded relatively easily. It can then be submitted as an e-mail to the local studies staff who can look at the merits of inclusion.

As is mentioned in Chapter 4, it is beneficial when the librarian has enough knowledge of web design and HTML to maintain the links sections of their site themselves. The parent organisation (and its Information Technology department in particular) should enable the local studies librarian to have at least enough access to the server to update and amend the links site.

National level

Currently, individual libraries at a local level are good at recognising the importance of the plethora of national sources which contribute to local studies. These sources may include the Deposit Libraries (the British Library, the National Library of Scotland, the National Library of Wales, Trinity College, Dublin, the Bodleian Library, Oxford and the Cambridge University Library) not to mention the Public Record Office (now part of the National Archives), the National Archives of Scotland, the General Register Office and the Public Record Office of Northern Ireland (PRONI). Many library websites provide links to these collections and sources. However, this does not always work well in reverse with less attention having been paid by the large, national institutions to what is held at a local level. This is perhaps inevitable given the very patchy nature of Internet coverage for local studies through the United Kingdom and, in many cases, the lack of details about the extent, scope and treatment of subjects within collections. This is one area that is ripe for serious web-based developments and, to a certain extent, the intiative must come from the local studies libraries on the ground – who perhaps need to shout about their collections more loudly in cyberspace simply in order to compete with the huge number of other sources and services clamouring for attention on the World Wide Web.

Archives and museums

To most people there appears to be an obvious link between the work of local studies librarians and archivists and also in many cases with the work of museum curators. These collections appear to be inextricably linked and interdependent, especially within the local context. In the past, it might be argued, however, that this seemingly obvious truth sometimes appears to be much more apparent to users than it is to professionals. In the past there has been much mutual suspicion between archivists and librarians; they are separate professions, with separate qualifications and separate approaches to managing knowledge. Although somewhat tongue-in-cheek, Martin Hayes, the Principal Librarian for Local Studies in West Sussex, described cooperation between archivists and librarians as 'sleeping with the enemy'.[1]

However tongue-in-cheek this might be it does betray the suspicions which still abound between the two groups of professionals. Yet, at the end of the day, archivists and local studies librarians are very much in the same business – preserving and facilitating access to the collective memories of their communities. Much of this book has focused on the idea that joined-up thinking is essential for local studies to prosper in the brave, new digital world. Perhaps nowhere is this more obviously the case than in the relationship between local studies libraries and archives. To the user, whether in person or remotely, distinctions between the role of, and service provision by, archives and local studies libraries seems scarcely important. Users want accurate information and they are not particularly concerned who supplies it. The ease with which the Internet has made information accessible is something that users fully expect from the other services they approach. However, this is not always as simple as it appears.

Some might claim that the situation is peculiarly bad in the public sector. Within the academic sector cooperation is often much closer with fewer of the distinctions between local collections, special collections and archives that tend to predominate elsewhere. Yet, on the surface at least cooperation within the public sector should be no more difficult. It is very often the case that public libraries, museums and archives may all fall within the remit of a department encompassing leisure or recreation; in some cases they may have one central manager or director. In Kent, Oxford and Suffolk, libraries and archives have become one department. This integrated approach has very much been emphasised by Re:source which encompasses all three elements. Re:source does foster mutual support between the three areas without suggesting the wholesale adoption of unified local studies or heritage centres, an approach which is more common in urban areas and in North America but one which is not without its vocal critics who argue that 'synergism' (bringing together similar units) has been discredited as an approach.

Hayes, speaking of his own experiences in West Sussex, described the need to make resolute efforts to achieve this 'seamless' thread. The Internet offers huge possibilities for cooperation between the archives and the local studies department. The two services may not want to have a combined web presence but this should not be dismissed out of hand. The beauty of the Internet is that two distinct services can be brought together relatively painlessly by the creation of a single homepage for both services. This does not compromise the two services and they can still retain their own individual websites but it does clearly bring the two services together in the minds of users and broadens their information-gathering experience. Such mechanisms, however, only really work if they go beyond a simple homepage and if links to the other service are embedded throughout the site. In this respect it returns to the importance of recognising complementary collections.

In terms of the content and style of website provision it should similarly be self-evident that librarians and archivists should work together. In the first instance they should collaborate on adopting a common house style throughout their respective sites. Some may argue that this is superficial and meaningless but to the user, both actual and virtual, this will reinforce the idea of a coherent service that cooperates and complements. In most cases, the house style will be dictated by the parent organisation, either a local authority or academic institution. However, archivists and librarians should seize the opportunity to create a common approach to informing the public about their sources and how to access their materials. The layout and navigation of the sites should be as similar as possible.

Inevitably, websites for special collections exist to indicate the scope and content of the collection. They are often disappointingly weak at providing users with assistance or guidance on how to access other, related materials. In the digital age there can be little excuse for this. This highlights the need for collaboration not only between archivists and librarians within one organisation but with those further afield as well. For example, a county record office might well possess the estate papers of a prominent family from the local gentry, while their personal papers may be in the local university's care and the photographs of the estate may be in the local studies department. It is in the interests of all three organisations to work together, identify what Hayes calls the seamless thread[2] and, with the aid of some simple hyperlinks, reunite the materials. However, the simplicity, perhaps even the banality of this statement obscures the very real practical difficulties that need to be overcome if a more fully integrated approach is to be taken.

The technological knowledge exists already but the Internet facilitates a more concerted approach and one which will ultimately benefit users. The materials themselves need not be digitised but the ability to get an immediate description of extent or scope or to search a catalogue from one terminal – whether within or without the library itself – is an attainable approach that demonstrates joined-up service delivery.

It is inevitable that cataloguing and stock management systems will be different for archives and local studies libraries as librarians and archivists have very different approaches to the organisation of knowledge and sources. Providing electronic access to the catalogues of local studies collections and archives should be addressed collectively, even if the cataloguing techniques and stock management software differ. Full integration of the catalogues of local studies and archives (and often of the museum service as well) is difficult and projects aiming to achieve this have often run into trouble. It has been suggested that in order to overcome some of the problems museums and local studies collections need to adopt the same level of description as archives.[3] The major benefit of electronic catalogues is remote access and catalogues need to be compliant with the Z39.50 standard for the interconnection of computers. Integrated catalogues of library collections already exist with none more successful that COPAC (*http://www.copac.ac.uk*) which provides simultaneous searching of the library OPACs of the Consortium of University Research Libraries (CURL). It is possible also to include catalogues for other collections. So far this has happened more extensively in the United States where the role of the local studies collection in the public library service may sometimes be eclipsed by that of the state historical society. An example mentioned by Hume and Lock is that of the Minnesota Historical Society Library whose catalogues are included on the Minnesota libraries network.[4]

Additionally, if an e-reference service is offered for local studies then the same facility should be available for users of the archives. Indeed, a common e-reference service for local studies and archives might be a more efficient possibility. A cooperative approach to enquiries was introduced in West Sussex long before the surge in Internet usage:

> A co-ordinated approach to enquiry-solving has also been developed. Letters received by the Library Service requesting substantial research (i.e. more than the half an hour offered free by library staff) are routinely passed to WSRO [West Sussex Records Office] to be tackled by their fee-based research service.[5]

If such an accommodation was possible in the days when most enquiries came by post or telephone then it would seem likely that e-mail would not unduly complicate the process. West Sussex Libraries provide an integrated online enquiry submission form for the local studies and county record office.

The active publication of current awareness bulletins or newsletters should be encouraged. Clearly, there is scope for archives and local studies to cooperate on this as so many of their sources overlap and to produce jointly issues of such a publication two or three times a year. The cost of production may well be offset by such collaboration and it will certainly ensure wider dissemination. This should not, however, be viewed simply as being for users but also to keep other members of staff within the other parts of the service abreast of current developments. Current awareness bulletins need not be hugely elaborate – a four-page bulletin can be produced relatively easily, more so if archives and local studies collaborate. Very often, services do produce excellent current awareness bulletins, guides to sources and services, annotated reading lists, handbooks to particular collections or leaflets on how to undertake local investigations such as 'tracing your roots' in a particular area. These can easily be converted into HTML and then uploaded to a central point of the organisation's server. They can then easily be linked to the archives and local studies alike. Many archives and local studies departments have a wide range of this type of grey literature which, with a little imagination and work, could become attractive and useful webpages to the benefit of both services. It should not, however, be a case of simply taking leaflets and converting them verbatim as this seldom leads to useful or attractive web pages. A little imagination and creativity goes a long way.

Academic community

On the whole, academic libraries do not view local studies in the same way as the public sector. It is not the function of an academic library simply to replicate the kinds of collections held in the public sector. In the first instance, academic libraries may not possess, necessarily, the neatly defined geographical limitations that apply in the public sector, consequently making stock selection less straightforward. In the past the litmus test for inclusion of material was to support teaching and research within the parent institution. In some cases, significant local collections have only been developed within academic institutions where there is perceived to be an absence of available materials elsewhere within the local community. No significant study has been undertaken on local studies with the libraries of the academic community since the mid-1980s.[6]

However, it is important to look to the whole of the academic community rather than to the more narrow focus of (just) academic libraries. There exist a number of specialist centres or institutes within universities that deal with aspects of community studies in general or history in particular. The English Local History Collection at Leicester University, the Rural History Centre at Reading University and the Elphinstone Institute at the University of Aberdeen are good examples of such institutions. The last-mentioned example, the Elphinstone Institute, reinforces the university's position in the north and north-east of Scotland and provides considerable amounts of material on the history and, perhaps more significantly, the culture and particularly the dialect of the region which is the principal defining characteristic of the local area.

This is an important point: some universities are perceived to be a central part of the cultural and economic, not to mention educational, life of a particular geographical region. This may be reflected within the library collection through the development of a local studies collection that is broader in its scope than the more narrow definition taken by public libraries in the region. Consequently, the university's collection may contain many sources that are useful to users of public library local collections. In Aberdeen's case this means that the local collection basically reflects the entire north-east of Scotland, a much wider remit than that of the individual local authorities that provide coverage of the area.

Having said this, it is also important to point out that, in many cases, local societies and organisations often have weaker links to academic institutions compared with stronger links with local studies departments in public libraries. This is perhaps partly responsible for the relatively small number of deposits of collections belonging to local groups within academic libraries. However, all of this is not to say that there exists no potential areas for collaboration. Indeed quite the reverse can be the case. Perhaps the principal strength of many academic collections lies in their possession of special collections (for example, the entire library of a local society or individual) and in their archive collections (estate records, personal papers, business archives to name but a few).

In the early days of digitisation, financial assistance was more forthcoming for projects to digitise materials in academic special collections than it was for similar activities in the public sector. This has changed since the advent of *Virtually New* and some might argue that the pendulum has swung too far in the opposite direction. Nevertheless, in the first phase of digitisation within the academic community, a great deal of useful material was made available to a much wider audience. In addition, the universities involved in digitisation projects have, by and large, produced a number of useful retrospective evaluations and appraisals of projects which offer constructive lessons for others considering this approach irrespective of sector.

Developing close relationships between the public and academic sector at a professional level is very important. Some users are likely to be reticent about approaching academic libraries because they may possess a certain mystique about them. Academic libraries, however, are making their collections more accessible (partly in response to initiatives on lifelong learning and the provision of services to remote users or distance learners). Given that local studies in both the academic and public sectors are essentially complementary, some very helpful partnerships can be created, with the sharing of electronic reources a prominent feature. At a very basic level, many local studies collections in the public sector would benefit enormously from providing, through their website, a link to enable users to search the local university catalogue, especially if a separate catalogue for special, local or archival collections exists. Aberdeen University Library's digitisation of the collection of nineteenth-century photographs by George Washington Wilson has created an electronic resource that is of huge historical and cultural benefit not only for the university community but for the wider community as well. Similarly, with Strathclyde University's Glasgow Digital Library, a significant resource has been created for the wider community. Public library local studies departments should be exploiting the activities of their academic colleagues for the benefit of users.

Community groups

Local studies are not simply the domain of the library. Rather the library is there to facilitate the work of others, whether individuals or organisations. It is undeniably vital that local studies librarians maintain close working relationships with other professionals in related fields but it is equally important they maintain very close links with those organisations in the community and, in many, cases individuals. Many of these will be organisations that are very familiar to the local studies librarian as their members may often be users of the collection. The wise local studies librarian does not underestimate the often astonishing level of knowledge or understanding which these groups or individuals may have about a particular facet of the community. Similarly, local studies staff should always recognise the limitations of their own knowledge and sources and, whenever possible, tap into this well of knowledge and expertise.

It is often the case that the role of the local studies librarian (with regard to heritage groups or historical societies within their local community) is considered to be confined to providing advice on how these organisations should maintain their own collections or attempting to secure the deposit of parts of their collections in the libraries. This interpretation alone presents a very one-sided, perhaps even mercenary approach. The strength of these organisations tends to lie in the fact that many of them have been in existence for a considerable time and they have, through their grassroots connections, built up considerable amounts of information of a type that it is difficult for the library to access. Additionally, many of them rely heavily on retired people who have the time to devote to an in-depth investigation of a particular subject.

Such organisations provide immeasurable benefits to their communities and to the collective understanding of their communities. If the local studies library is the collective memory of the community then these organisations, proactively researching their subjects, must really be seen almost as the brain of the community. Many of these organisations will have had a long tradition of producing short and often cheaply priced publications about particular aspects of local life. More and more, however, they are turning to the Internet (while often still maintaining their traditional hard-copy publishing) as a cheaper tool for disseminating their information.

The onus must be on the librarian to keep in regular contact with such organisations and make concerted, indeed determined, efforts to interact with these groups and to provide users of details about them when appropriate. Many libraries, particularly but not exclusively in the public sector, maintain files or even databases of local organisations. The Internet offers the potential to provide these services electronically and thus remotely whether as a searchable database or as a more straightforward alphabetical listing. Such a service can be annotated with the organisation providing a brief description of their purpose. If mounted on the Internet such a service can make direct links to organisations' homepages as well as providing e-mail contacts. Given that many libraries attempt to update such lists regularly to maintain accuracy the inclusion of this on a website would be an undeniably useful feature. However, this is not being usefully exploited in many cases. One local studies librarian made the dubious claim that he 'knew about every local website' but yet there is no evidence on this library's homepage that they have been collected together systematically and made available for the public.[7]

Eventually, it may even possible for local studies departments to attempt to e-enable these groups. Local studies departments have often provided space within the library for community organisations to mount small-scale exhibitions. The same may be done in cyberspace. It need not necessarily be a virtual exhibition as mentioned earlier but it may be a brief description of the organisation's activities. One mechanism may be to provide a single web page to those groups which have not managed to establish their own Internet presence to enable them to describe briefly their aims and functions and to provide membership and contact details. A number of sites provide such a service for commercial or voluntary organisations (for example, sites such as Church Net UK (*http://www*

.churchnet.org.uk) enable churches with websites to enter a brief description together with their URL). Local studies websites should definitely attempt to replicate this.

Inevitably, such a strategy requires careful management. In the first instance, the editorial control and uploading must remain, at all times, with the librarian or the service's webmaster. It is also important to give very careful consideration to the sort of group that will be allowed to contribute details. It will almost certainly be necessary to exclude pressure groups, those that are either overtly or covertly political or those with perhaps more dubious preoccupations. However, if this is handled sensibly this should not cause a problem. In spite of this book (and almost every other concerned with local studies) stressing that local studies is much more than simply local history, it might be prudent to provide the opportunity for a web page only to organisations that are involved in local history (although this definition can be sufficiently wide to enable the inclusion of a wide range of organisations covering not only the purely historical but also those interested in archaeological, topographical, literary or scientific subjects as well).

The issue of e-enabling these groups is perhaps something broader than the scope of a work concerned solely with local studies. Community bulletin boards may be another area in which there is scope for potential. If a library has a noticeboard for posters then why not an electronic equivalent? Local studies departments, with their excellent links to the community and its organisations, are perhaps in an ideal place to coordinate and encourage among these groups a better understanding of the benefits of the information superhighway. This can be done by providing resource lists for local groups considering a web presence, including examples of good practice or step-by-step guidelines to web design and content creation. This may sound daunting and time-consuming but the material is already out there in cyberspace and it is simply a case of identifying it and linking it together. As the traditional link between education and the library is being reinforced more and more, the library as a whole could consider running Internet training sessions for local organisations. These would not, as a matter of necessity, be concerned with web design and creation, but more with the benefits of being part of the Internet revolution. The potential is endless.

Individuals

One area which is often neglected in terms of collaboration and cooperation is the potential benefits of working with private individuals or, perhaps, more accurately the benefits of individuals working on behalf of the community. Many of these individuals will probably be well known to the local studies department staff as regular users of the collection. However, sometimes if these are 'seasoned' users of the collection their reliance on interaction from the library professionals will be limited; they will be thoroughly familiar with the multiplicity of sources and will, perhaps, have relatively little cause to ask the library staff anything. This can result in the local studies staff perhaps missing some golden opportunities to benefit from the researches of individuals.

There are numerous instances of individuals who have investigated the history of their village or their ancestry to an astonishingly professional degree. In some instances they may work with other local or family historians but without ever formalising their collaboration as part of family history or local history societies. Increasingly, for many people who have systematically and often dogmatically researched family and community history in this fashion, the Internet is offering an easy, cheap, effective and efficient method of disseminating their researches in a way that publishing a monograph cannot.

In this particular digital environment, one of the principal tasks of any local studies library should be the methodical identification of the webmasters of as many local websites as possible. Many will probably be known to them but the librarian should also ascertain whether these webmasters would be happy to deal with the referral of some enquiries. Obvious judgements about the appropriateness of this have to be made on an individual basis (both in terms of the librarian and the webmaster). However, many local history webmasters are keen to deal with such enquiries (in the same way as they enthusiastically deal with enquiries sent directly to them) because remote enquiries often lead to the exchange of information and assist in completing another part of the jigsaw of local or family history.

In recent years, there has been an increased emphasis, in more general digital reference service terms, to approaching subject experts in order to provide responses to particular enquiries. There is no reason why this approach should not be replicated in local studies. Such collaboration is often a very helpful and efficient method of dealing with enquiries which might otherwise involve library staff in long and protracted investigations. There may well be instances when enquiries, particularly genealogical ones, can be answered more fully by a layman who has spent years investigating a particular family or location than by a librarian who cannot hope to have the same level of knowledge.

An interesting example of this can be found with the Port Gordon Local History website (*http://www.portgordon.org/*) which deals with the history of a small village in the north of Scotland (see Figure 6.1). In addition to the historical content of the site, the webmaster has compiled pedigrees of all the families in the village since its establishment in 1797. Several hundred pages of narrative genealogies have been created. In addition to providing genealogical data, the webmaster has also created a collection of supplementary documents. A digital archive of old photographs has also been created and is constantly being added to. This has involved input from the local studies library which has enabled the inclusion of their old photographs of the village (or at least the inclusion of those for which the library owns the copyright). Perhaps more significant, however, has been the systematic digitisation of old photographs of former inhabitants of the village with locals happily allowing their old photographs to be digitised. In addition, some privately-owned primary sources have also been digitised. All of this has been undertaken by an individual local historian.

The local studies librarian for the area is well aware of both the site in general and the genealogical materials behind it and the webmaster is happy to deal with referrals of enquiries about the village or the genealogies. The webmaster of this site is happy to share information but emphasises that he does not provide a research service and will not undertake primary research on behalf of remote users. Since the launch of the site, there have been enquiries from descendants of villagers from the United States, Canada, Australia, New Zealand, Italy and around the United Kingdom. Indeed, the webmaster himself found a long-lost third cousin as a result of a referral from the local studies librarian.

Figure 6.1   Port Gordon Local History Online

Reproduced courtesy of Port Gordon Local History Online. Available at *http://www. portgordon.org/*.

Conclusion: issues and concerns

There are, however, a number of issues associated with this sort of collaboration. Perhaps the most important is connected with the quality and reliability of the information contained in private websites. This has to be examined carefully and evaluated to the best abilities of the librarian because the quality of the response may reflect on the library service. Questions of reliability, validity and accuracy need to be addressed. The Port Gordon Local History site is a good example because the webmaster is both a librarian and a historian but other sites may be less rigorous. The potential dangers in referrals to 'amateurs', no matter how dedicated or enthusiastic, must indicate extreme caution. It is also important to remember that private individuals (or indeed private societies or organisations) are not bound by the performance indicators that the library may adhere to. The library may strive to provide a response to an enquiry within two working days or within a week but a private local site may not have a formalised policy and may take some considerable time to get back to an enquirer. Consequently, the librarians needs to bear this in mind because nothing irks an enquirer more than the apparent ignoring of a request for information.

The fluidity of the Internet is also potentially a big problem, particularly with private individuals or organisations who may change their Internet Service Provider or their e-mail address(es) without thinking of informing the library. The stronger the links that the local studies librarian has with the local community the easier it becomes to implement some informal method of electronic deposit (at least in terms of electronic contact details if not subject material).

Having said that, partnership is the way forward whether it is through liaison on an informal level or through formal collaborative ventures. Much of the groundwork has already been done and many collaborative projects undertaken in the shape of exhibitions, dealing with enquiries and referrals, resource sharing and staff training. The Internet will not change that. Rather it will simply provide a new medium and make easier long-distance collaboration and cooperation, enabling local studies libraries to remain both relevant and dynamic to the widest possible audience.

Notes

1. Martin Hayes (1997) 'Sleeping with the enemy', *Local Studies Librarian*, 16(1): 2.
2. Hayes, 'Sleeping with the enemy', p. 2.
3. L.E. Sherwood (1998) 'Discovering the buffalo story robes: a case for cross domain information strategies', *Computers and the Humanities*, 32: 57–64.
4. Eileen Hume and Alice Lock (2002) 'Information access and retrieval', in Michael Dewe (ed.), *Local Studies Collection Management*. Aldershot: Ashgate, p. 109.
5. Hayes, 'Sleeping with the enemy', p. 4.
6. Although at the time of going to press a funded research proposal had been submitted by one UK library school.
7. Private source.

E-learning

Introduction

Information and communication technology has affected not only libraries. It has made a significant impact on the education sector and on pedagogical approaches and methods, although many believe that much more research is required on the true nature of this impact. ICT has substantively altered the way in which teaching is delivered and learning is undertaken across all sectors of education from primary through to tertiary levels. This explosion in the application of technology has been mirrored by a rejuvenated enthusiasm, exhibited within the National Curriculum and elsewhere, for local studies. The aim of this chapter is, therefore, to bring these two strands together and examine how, within the local studies context, the digital age has affected the way in which the library assists the teaching and learning process. In the United Kingdom, both the National Curriculum and the National Grid for Learning within the United Kingdom have reinforced the importance of local history. In many respects, this brings the UK more fully into line with guiding principles elsewhere in the English-speaking world where local history has always had a central place in the curriculum.

This chapter outlines the links which exist between local studies collections and the education sector at all levels and emphasises the importance of creating constructive and beneficial alliances between librarians and educators. The chapter also addresses how the Internet can be harnessed to maintain these alliances and relationships. In addition, the chapter also examines the methods that may be adopted for encouraging those in the education sector – both teachers and students – to play a constructive part in content creation through community digital archives. Examples of good practice are examined, including sites such as *Focus On … The Census* and the *Powys Digital History Project*, and the methods that sites such as these use to make local studies materials more accessible to, and interesting for, the younger generation.

Those involved in teaching and learning – whether as educators or students – have long made use of the resources available within local studies collections. As with the reference library in general, the local studies department has an intrinsic appeal to those studying. Local studies departments have practised lifelong learning and social inclusion for decades, long before these terms became the 'buzzwords' for a modern and successful library service. The inclusive nature of local studies departments stems partly from the sheer diversity of materials available, partly because the local angle can often make investigations seem less daunting and more relevant and partly because of the proactive approach of staff working in local studies who have, in many cases, reached out into the community through liaison with groups, societies, organisations and individuals.

This has been a truly inclusive approach because it has never been restricted to those who are in formal education but has included those who are essentially self-improvers, whether working under their own auspices or as part of some open learning or evening-class programme. Increasingly, however, the explosion in use of online technologies is being seen as providing an opportunity to reach out further into the community, with particular emphasis placed on how these technologies can be harnessed to attract non-users. The opportunities offered by ICT have been seized not only by libraries but by those in the educational sector as well. Internet-based resources for schoolchildren are widely used and many central government initiatives seek to capitalise on this. In tertiary education also, the Internet has become both a serious research tool and a major aid to teaching and learning through the development of virtual learning environments (VLEs).

At the same time as these technological developments have occurred, so too has more emphasis been placed on the notion of local investigations within education (at all levels and in all sectors). Local topics are seen as being accessible and relevant to students and are viewed as a good tool for developing an understanding of major, even global, issues, whether that be the impact of the Second World War or an environmental issue. This has resulted in local studies collections being viewed as key participants in the learning experience. This may be nothing new but it does, perhaps, mean that the role of local studies departments is now more visible than it was previously.

Changes to the curriculum have resulted in schoolchildren both at primary and secondary levels being required to carry out some sort of local investigation. Sometimes, the perception of the role of local studies is rather superficial and considered to be largely limited to local history and that other subjects are, for the most part, marginalised. Practitioners rightly reject this assertion even if their collections are strongly historically orientated. The impact of local studies within the secondary school curriculum is not limited purely to history. Use of a local studies collection is just as likely to be a central component in projects for subjects such as economics or business, leisure or tourism, geography or sociology as it is for a historical investigation. The local studies collection also offers considerable scope for the examination of issues such as the democratic process at work and the administration of justice both of which may be said to be core to the recently articulated desire to create more 'well-rounded' citizens.

Local investigations and community-based research are not restricted to the school system. As the previous chapter outlines, universities and colleges have also adopted this approach and some institutions have been involved in local history since the 1940s. Further and higher education institutions are not simply teaching local history; they are, in some cases, teaching *how to study* local history. Often such courses are taught by distance learning, meaning that students enrolled in the programme may make use of the local studies collection within their own vicinity. Such a mode of delivery has helped to open up education and attract individuals who might not otherwise have considered further study.

Open and distance learning at the tertiary level has expanded dramatically since the mid to late 1990s, with many higher education institutions attempting to create fully virtual universities. Experience in running technology-based open and distance learning programmes is more widespread in the United States than it is in the United Kingdom. Similarly, academic libraries with local collections tend to be more sophisticated in their approach to the Internet in the United States. Until relatively recently, the Open University was almost the only institution in the United Kingdom involved in the design and delivery of technology-based distance learning.

The adoption of VLEs[1] and the desire to recreate in cyberspace the 'university experience' or the campus has been done largely in response to the concepts of lifelong learning and social inclusion which have figured so prominently in recent library thinking. In some respects, higher education institutions have had to think more seriously about how to do this than local studies departments which have a strong tradition of meeting these two requirements. In the education sector, VLEs are perceived as a medium for broadening access to teaching and learning and thus ultimately fulfilling the twin objectives of lifelong learning and social inclusion. However, that is not to say that VLEs have been received with universal approval by those in the sector. Some question the time required to create and maintain materials on virtual learning environments, some question the lack of appreciation for work being done in this medium while others question the pedagogical implications and whether these have been addressed in any meaningful way. In spite of this, enthusiasm for these new technologies has led some institutions to convert their conventional hard-copy distance learning programmes into a digital format; in other instances entirely new courses have come on stream designed specifically for virtual delivery.

The expansion opportunities that the Internet offers means that students may now be located anywhere and that it is no longer necessary 'to go away to university'. While these virtual students will, invariably, have access to and make regular use of the library service of the institution that they are studying at, they may also make more demands on their own home library service for the sake of simple convenience.[2] This has implications for the public library service in general. Given that this expansion in open and distance learning has been mirrored by an increased interest in local history as a discipline, it is entirely likely that local studies departments will, in the not too distant future, be confronted with an increased demand from this sector of the community. Given the increasing prevalence of VLEs and 'virtual universities' which aim to make learning more flexible and responsive to students' circumstances, it is likely that this particular user group will have much higher expectations about the quality and range of the service. These heightened expectations will particularly manifest themselves in terms of digital services and the provision of electronic (and remotely accessible) electronic sources. If it is possible to study for a degree over the Internet, these users are likely to view local libraries that do not respond to the electronic environment unsympathetically. Within the remit of this book, local studies departments that simply provide a brief outline of their collection on their website are not going to be viewed favourably by increasingly sophisticated and 'e-enabled' users.

Responding to the very different demands of these diverse user groups is potentially a difficult task; adult learners have very different expectations from children in primary school but, increasingly, all of these user groups do have electronic expectations. However, e-learning within the local studies context is not simply restricted to those who are involved in education (whether formal or informal). It is equally about providing users with an understanding of the sources and how they fit together to provide the answers that they may be looking for. E-learning within local studies is also about providing basic information literacy in order to make users aware of the problems and pitfalls as well as the benefits and advantages of using both the sources in-house and those available electronically through the Internet. The Internet is perhaps the most effective tool for providing users with this understanding through online tutorials and by encouraging them to examine and appraise sites and sources in a way that conventional hard-copy leaflets or pamphlets cannot do.

Liaison

At the outset, local studies staff should seek to identify all the potential stakeholders in this process. Although it may be argued that this could, perhaps, be covered more generically as part of general collaboration and cooperation, it is, in fact, something much more specific. In reality, meaningful collaboration and cooperation with the education sector requires much more thought and possibly even a formal learning strategy or education policy. An integral part of such a strategy must be consideration of the most efficient and effective use of information and communications technology in general and the Internet in particular.

Local studies collections have always maintained an appeal for those involved in education whether that is primary, secondary or tertiary or whether it is formal education or informal self-improvement. With the advent of the Internet, the sharing of resources between stakeholders is made more easy and more effective. Initially, however, it is necessary to identify clearly who those stakeholders are and understand their requirements in terms of local studies subject provision. Don Martin in his *Local Studies Libraries Guidelines* highlights this point when he says:

> It is important that relationships are forged between local studies librarians and education staff involved in local studies work, at all levels.[3]

It is particularly important that local studies staff make good contacts with all local school libraries who will assist in the process of fostering relationships with teachers and classes. It is equally important to attempt to contact directly those teachers who have recently made use of the collection as well.

The changes to the school curriculum which have seen an increased prominence attached to local studies and local investigations has not been without difficulties. One of the most significant worries is the fact that many primary school staff have no training in history and lack an understanding of the sources, either individually or collectively, and consequently have felt uncomfortable about teaching the subject. Equally, some secondary school history teachers may not necessarily be all that familiar with *local* history sources either: since the curriculum was, until relatively recently, more focused on national or world history. In these circumstances teachers may well turn initially to the school librarian. However, the school librarian may also not be familiar with local studies sources or there may be no school librarian to turn to and consequently the focus of the educators' attentions becomes the local studies department itself.

For many years local studies departments have been involved with school-level education in the form of visiting schools within the area, encouraging students (either individually or as part of class visits) to come and see the collection itself, by the production of resources aimed at either teachers or students or by participating in training for staff. In many cases, this has led to local studies departments formulating their own education policies which have formalised the approaches outlined above. Such a formal structure is recommended by Don Martin as a mechanism for ensuring that local studies provides exactly what the education service is looking for.

It is perhaps regrettable that hitherto much of the emphasis in fostering these relationships has been restricted to primary and secondary education. It is equally important to foster links with tertiary-level education, whether further or higher education. The potential for collaboration and cooperation with academic libraries in the local area has been touched upon in Chapter 6. However, this should be taken further and closer contacts fostered with appropriate departments. In the first instance, it is likely that this will be history departments but in the longer term more widespread contacts should be the aim.

These contacts may result in very beneficial alliances such as the sharing of resources and increased use of the collection by students as academics become more aware of what is available and thus encourage students to undertake investigations with more of a local focus. It may well also lead to collaborative projects. However, in some respects, establishing contacts with tertiary-level education institutions has become a more challenging area with the explosion in Internet usage and with the advent of virtual learning environments (as outlined earlier in this chapter). Local residents may well be enrolled on distance learning courses hosted by institutions based remotely. It becomes much more difficult to identify and assess the potential needs of these users. Don Martin states 'the requirements of Open University students should also be borne in mind'.[4] This is true, but now there are many other institutions offering open and distance learning programmes and it is difficult for the librarian to access this sector. Distance learning (both conventional and online) is far more advanced in the United States (as the wealth of literature on online learning demonstrates by its US orientation). As a consequence, academic libraries in the United States have much greater experience serving users at a distance and public libraries have a heightened awareness of the potential needs of this user community. Librarians need to start becoming more familiar with online learning provision through examination of organisations such as the British Association for Online

Learners (BAOL). User surveys should also be used as a means to identify those engaged in distance learning.

A number of dynamic projects have resulted from closer collaboration with tertiary-level education, not least the involvement of Liverpool University in the creation of the Knowsley website. Similarly, Gateshead Libraries, perhaps one of the most innovative in the United Kingdom, are working in conjunction with Newcastle University to provide online tuition about family history using Blackboard. Blackboard along with WebCT are two of the main platforms for creating virtual learning environments. Their use within the library sector is very much in its infancy.

The creation of online tuition for family history points up another significant user community that requires some attention in terms of e-learning, namely those self-improvers who are not enrolled in any formal education programme but for whom the whole experience of working with the sources in a local studies department is a valuable and hugely enjoyable learning experience. This is a user community that must not be forgotten and the implementation of any e-learning strategies must bear this group in mind and attempt to cater for their needs.

The process of liaison should be a learning process for both librarian and educator. The librarian should learn about the likely resource requirements and demands to be made on the collection and the educators should learn about the sources and services. In some cases, a specific member of staff may be appointed to carry out this liaison. Increasingly, however, if an individual is to be appointed to oversee this sort of liaison, it is important that they have at least a basic understanding of web-based developments and how the Internet may be used most advantageously. As well as liaising with those in the education sector it is important also to look at the other staff within the library service and to bring them fully into any discussions too. Children's or young people's librarians may have a particular insight to offer and, equally importantly, the information technologists will be able to provide advice on the practicalities of ideas. Individual staff may have an understanding of pedagogy which may prove to be useful.

Online tuition

Jill Barber has pointed out that many local studies collections now run services tailored specifically to the schools within their area.[5] However, this is often still largely focused towards the conventional forms of interaction between libraries and schools – visits, resource packs, exhibitions and the like. Consideration of online content creation or online tuition is still often at a fairly basic level, if it exists at all. This is unfortunate because, increasingly, schoolchildren – and often those from a very young age – are familiar and comfortable with information technology in general and the Internet in particular. As a result, library websites have sought consciously to appeal to this market. For local studies collections, which have so much to offer to those in education, it is particularly important to give active consideration to Internet-based resources for this audience and, more specifically, to focus sections of the local studies department's website on this market.

Libraries in general and public libraries in particular are now being viewed as a focal point within the community to facilitate learning and are, in many instances, eagerly endorsing their roles as resource centres in support of lifelong learning. Given this, online tuition and e-learning strategies are perhaps one of the most important areas for digital content development and creation.

It would be foolish and naive to state that all local studies departments are in a position either financially or technologically to produce sophisticated, animated, interactive websites. It would be even more foolish to suggest that all libraries can create the highly sophisticated type of sites that children are increasingly coming to expect in order to sustain their interest and enthusiasm. However, the beauty of the Internet lies in the fact that the organisation itself does not need to – there are many excellent websites in existence which can be harnessed to assist in delivering teaching and learning. Equally, from the perspective of the local studies department, it need not necessarily rely exclusively on in-house productions to explain its resources and how what information they contain on many web-based resources will already serve the purpose. Ultimately, there is little point in librarians reinventing the wheel.

Users of all descriptions require help and assistance with the sources and how to access them and make sense of the information contained within them. For many years, libraries have often produced this type of material in hard-copy format for users. However, as with so many other areas of local studies service provision, the Internet can offer a range of new opportunities, not least in removing the previous reliance on these in-house guides to sources or 'tutorial support' (which may often have been rather dull affairs). Perhaps the major benefit of the Internet is the ability with one click of the mouse to connect to a remote site which may offer a unique insight into a particular subject or issue. Other organisations may well have produced web-based guides to sources or even highly interactive tutorials which show the user how a particular source or service operates. One of the best examples of e-learning about local studies sources has been produced not by a local studies library but by the UK Public Record Office (now part of the National Archives) with its Learning Curve initiative and, in particular, its site *Focus On ... The Census* (see Figure 7.1).

Figure 7.1 *Focus On ... The Census*

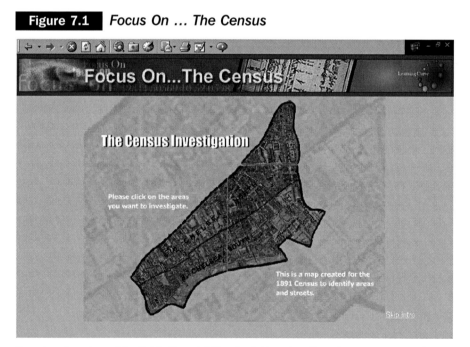

Reproduced courtesy of the Public Record Office. Available at *http://learningcurve.pro.gov.uk/ FocusOn/census/intro.htm*.

Focus On ... The Census: online learning

The fact that *Focus On ... The Census* has been produced by the PRO rather than an individual local studies department is perhaps not surprising. Certainly, when the site is explored its sophistication, design and interaction are highly appealing and commendable, and few individual library authorities in the public sector would have the resources to spare for this kind of provision. However, the PRO is in a good position to create a site like this and both the library and education communities in the United Kingdom and beyond can reap the benefits. It also offers practitioners a valuable lesson in that it emphasises that the material is of direct relevance to local studies departments and their users and need not necessarily be created by or held in a local repository. Consequently, libraries across the globe can simply and easily link to a site like *Focus On ... The Census*.

Although *Focus On ... The Census* is primarily geared towards schoolchildren it provides a very useful introduction to the Census for anyone about to embark on using that source for the first time. Some of the tasks and animations are obviously directed at children and sustaining their interest but the text and images are interesting and informative and, above all, it presents in an easily digestible format what the Census is all about, how the various parts of it fit together and the types of information that can be obtained from it. For anyone consulting *Focus On ... The Census* it is difficult to resist the temptation to complete the quizzes and questions and to assess one's own abilities and understanding of the source. Encouraging users both in-house and remotely to spend ten minutes looking at *Focus On … The Census* before consulting the source itself may be time well spent and considerably less time-consuming and repetitive for staff. Yet it is perhaps an online tutorial tool that is not exploited as fully as it could be within local studies departments.

In this respect, the importance of local studies staff undertaking regular and thorough Internet searching cannot be underestimated. Very often, this is a difficult thing to find time to undertake but the systematic identification and retrieval of useful websites is a vitally important task. It is not, however, enough simply to bookmark these as favourites for the library staff; wider dissemination through a local studies links page is essential as users may very well lack both the searching and critical appraisal skills which library staff have and this is particularly true of schoolchildren. However beneficial the Internet may be for providing access to information there also exists a great deal of dubious and inaccurate material. Consequently, one of the central features of e-learning within the library context in general is the need to provide information literacy training. This is particularly significant within the context of local studies where the sources may very often be widely acknowledged to be partial, lacking in corroboration and in some cases inaccurate and unreliable. It is also important to show users how the disparate sources fit together to produce a wider picture.

One accusation that has been made against some local studies websites is that they primarily provide little more than an outline of the collection and the types of sources and services available. This outline is often superficial and sometimes the impression is given that it is written for people who already understand the sources and services with little thought to explaining the different sources and how they fit together. Clearly a remote tool such as *Focus On … The Census* has a role to play in enabling users to gain a deeper and more thorough understanding of that particular source.

However, relying exclusively on external websites does not necessarily address the problem nor does it counter accusations of superficiality. One useful mechanism to overcome this is the creation of a basic online tutorial which focuses on getting started in local studies research. This may indeed be focused around the basic description of the sources but supplemented by pop-up definitions to explain exactly what, for example, an Old Parish Register is. A number of points need to be borne in mind:

- Do not call it an online tutorial – use something more accessible and user-friendly like 'how to get started'.

- Remember that new users will require an explanation about local studies in general, and remember to explain terms that may seem obvious to professionals or regular users but which might baffle new users. For example, explain about microfilm and microfiche, and do not simply say that 'old newspapers are available on microfilm' – explain why.

- Use simple language and put labels on images or particular words in the text – use 'What is this?' rather than 'a definition'.

- Include an image of the source if at all possible as this will assist users to understand it.

- Clearly describe the type of information that each source can provide.

- Discuss the shortcomings of this source openly and comment on their causes – users do not want to be left wondering why the Old Parish Register may be inaccurate.

- Discuss the general problems of local studies including partial coverage and also difficulties with reading old sources but do not labour the point (users are generally not stupid).

- Remember to outline what the collection does not hold and provide guidance on where these sources may be obtained.

- On the final page provide a link to a print-friendly version of the tutorial (this may simply be a word-processed version but time needs to be devoted to getting this right).

If a single online tutorial is being created it needs to be kept at a reasonably generic level in order that it can be used by and appeal to the widest possible audience, from schoolchildren doing a project to retired people taking up a new hobby. Some level of interaction with the site is essential so that at the end of the process those working through the tutorial can feel that they have learned from the experience. An interactive test or quiz may be one solution but this needs to be kept on a general level. Software packages such as Tool Book can make this relatively easy.

There does, however, exist a particular issue with online tutorial help for children. In informational terms the support may need to be kept at a reasonably general level but many children will expect it to be lively and perhaps even interactive in order to sustain their interest. They may be looking for animations and be perfectly happy to navigate through a series of clicks of the mouse in a way that an older audience may be less comfortable with. Given this disparity it may become necessary to create a dedicated area for children. This is no bad thing if it broadens the appeal of the collection. It does, however, require very careful consideration and input from educators. Some library services have already tailored general services specifically to children. As has been mentioned, West Sussex Libraries' reference department has a specific online enquiry submission for children; it also provides examples of the type of questions that can be asked and encourages children to explore subjects that might, perhaps, be associated with their school work. In general, however, much more consideration needs to be given to the methods and approaches by which local studies departments can provide digital services specifically for children and young people. The confidence that the young have with ICT is often not matched by the practitioners and, ultimately, it is the service that suffers.

Online tuition about sources is, however, just one area which might be exploited. Another is the use of web-based technologies for delivering actual teaching and learning. This is not something which local studies departments can undertake on their own; it must be a partnership with other bodies and agencies. In any case, funding opportunities for such projects would largely be reliant on partnership or consortia approaches bringing together the stakeholders in the library and information community, those in the education community and those with technological know-how to make the project work.

Collaborative ventures do, however, offer significant potential for local studies departments. The Knowsley project is a case in point. It was not, however, principally focused at education or schoolchildren. Yet one of the most important opportunities that the Internet offers library services is that of increased accessibility to materials for children. In such circumstances, collaborative ventures are often viewed sympathetically by funding agencies such as the Heritage Lottery Funding.

Powys Digital History Project

One of the most innovative of recent projects directed at schools is the Powys Digital History Project/Prosiect Hanes Digidol Powys (*http://history.powys.org.uk/*) (see Figure 7.2). This project was supported by the Heritage Lottery Fund and is essentially a joint initiative involving Powys Education Department and Powys Community, Leisure and Recreation Department, with much of the content being supplied by the County Archives and Local Studies Library Service. It demonstrates how good local studies projects require the involvement of a number of agencies.

The site covers the local history of 18 communities in Powys (formerly the counties of Breconshire, Montgomeryshire and Radnorshire). The themes that the site covers include details on 'Victorian Powys for schools' and the 'Early Crime and Punishment project' which enables users to work through the case of the 'Newtown Three'. There also a wealth of material about individual communities and the local estates.

The site also includes background information for teachers about how to make the best of the resource within a classroom environment.

Figure 7.2   Powys Digital History Project home page

Reproduced courtesy of Powys County Council. Available at *http://history.powys.org .uk/history/intro/menu3.html*.

Projects such as Powys Digital History can only be undertaken through collaboration with other stakeholders. It does, however, highlight the potential value of such collaboration and shows clearly how local studies collections can be exploited in the digital environment to the great benefit of the education sector. Material which once might have seemed boring, difficult or inaccessible to schoolchildren can now become interesting, easy and interactive thanks to the Internet.

All of this highlights how essential it is that local studies staff work closely with their counterparts in the education sector. On a basic level such cooperation enables local studies departments to identify which subjects are likely to be investigated as part of the curriculum and attempt to respond in the most beneficial fashion. On a higher level, it may lead to ventures similar to that in Powys and, ultimately, enable the planning of digitisation projects.

All of this requires work, and promotional work at that. Don Martin in his *Local Studies Libraries Guidelines* highlights the importance of copies of promotional literature being sent to local schools, colleges and appropriate local university departments. This is correct but the advances in technology over recent years now require a more dynamic solution. The traditional hard-copy current awareness bulletin is likely still to exist but this should be mirrored within the website with a 'What's New' section. Jill Barber rightly asserts that the simple conversion of leaflets or pamphlets into web pages makes for dull viewing.[6] A 'What's New' section on the local studies department website is absolutely essential and should contain (basically) the same text as the hard-copy current awareness bulletin but with, perhaps, the addition of some appropriate images, hyperlinks or e-mail addresses.

However, this alone does not make for an entire electronic dissemination strategy. It is equally important to target current awareness bulletins directly to education staff, both school librarians and teachers. The advent of e-mail means that local studies staff can quickly and easily send out their regular current awareness bulletins. The local studies department should maintain a variety of e-mail distribution lists, one of which should include all local schools and colleges to ensure that updates can be disseminated easily and efficiently within the local community. Further, if the information technology infrastructure allows for it, a mechanism can be put in place whereby users can tick a box on screen to receive an automatic e-mail notifying them that the page has been updated. Similarly, an online mechanism to request copies of current awareness bulletins should be considered.

Some school libraries have deliberately sought to provide more in-depth coverage of local studies in-house. In the digital age, where the sharing of resources is made much easier, it is therefore essential to have good communication between the various service providers so that information about new sources or services can be spread quickly. Given the largely disorganised nature of the Internet and the reliance that inevitably still exists on serendipity, the ability to alert colleagues to new sites is important.

As well as involvement with collaborative ventures there should also be liaison with the stakeholders over initiatives that the local studies department wishes to undertake on its own. For example, local studies departments considering launching a digitisation project should consult with local stakeholders in general and with schools, colleges and universities in particular, and examine their input and feedback. If digitisation, whether of texts, photographs or maps, is being considered then it is vital that the opinions of staff in the education sector are sought. Those in education (at whatever level) will form a key audience and the value and merit of digitisation to them needs to be considered from a very early stage. It is likely that the ability to demonstrate educational merit to funding agencies will be advantageous in attempting to secure financial support either internally or externally.

Feedback and outcomes

Contact with educational stakeholders is not simply a one-way process in which the library reaches out and others receive. Feedback from these groups is essential. School visits to the department may well be used to explain sources and services on a face-to-face basis but they can, with a little creativity, be used to obtain users' opinions about the website provision. Given that schoolchildren on a visit are essentially a captive audience, local studies staff should endeavour to find out whether they have used the service's website, what they think about it and, perhaps more importantly, what they think should be on it. Often children are the most critical and will say the things that adults might couch in more diplomatic terms. Increasingly, children possess a good understanding of the Internet as well as of the attractiveness or usefulness of sites, and will express their opinions in a forthright and candid fashion. School visits can, therefore, almost be regarded as mini focus groups providing feedback that is just as valuable – and in many cases a good deal more frank – as that posted in guest-books or comments pages on the Web itself.

Nor should the interaction with the educational sector be a one-sided process in which the library simple provides the raw materials or the librarian acts as the conduit to sources. It is important that the local studies department attempts to harness the researches of others and seeks to obtain copies of their work for the collection. The Folkways Project (see Chapter 4) identifies the importance of emphasising to schoolchildren in particular that their investigations in local, community or family history may well be worthy of long-term preservation. Increasingly, the preservation of such projects in a digital form is easy and efficient and will in most cases particularly appeal to children. Folkways itself does archive school projects electronically and believes that the creation of a digital archive of school projects gives additional meaning to the work that the students have undertaken. There is also a certain appeal for children to have their work mounted on a website and the commitment to do so shows, in a meaningful fashion, that adults *do* believe in the abilities of children to carry out rigorous and scholarly research.

This can be taken a stage further and applied to university dissertations or theses. Indeed it may be more convenient for students to supply a copy of their investigations electronically than in hard copy. Such works can relatively easily be converted into HTML and uploaded once all the academic niceties of assessment have been completed. In this way, local studies departments are not only being seen to embrace the new technologies but are reaping rewards from the time and effort put into fostering closer ties with the education establishment. Ultimately, they are also increasing their own digital record and further widening access to both the subject in question and the local studies collection.

Conclusion

Given the inevitably narrow nature of local studies collections it is perhaps not surprising that little time and effort has been devoted to identifying digital resources further afield (excepting the major electronic sources such as Family Search). *Focus On ... The Census* shows how one site can offer a great deal of benefit to all collections that make use of the Census. In terms of e-learning and online tuition there is no point in reinventing the wheel and attempting to create in-house a tool that has already been developed elsewhere. It might well be suggested that one of the future areas for development is the establishment of a local studies gateway that incorporates individual websites for local studies as well as more generic materials that explain the sources in local studies and how they interact with one another.

Notes

1. A great deal has been written about virtual learning environments as a cursory glance at editions of the *Library Association Record/CILIP Update* since 2000 will demonstrate. Also, the work of the LTSN (the Learning and Teaching Support Network) and in particular the Centre for Information and Computer Sciences (*http://www.ics.ltsn.ac.uk/*) has significantly informed this area.

2. From personal experience running the distance learning MSc in Information and Library Studies at the Robert Gordon University, Aberdeen, this is clearly the case. Students on the programme make as much use of their local libraries as they do that of the university.

3. Don Martin (2002) *Local Studies Libraries*, 2nd edn. London: Library Association, p. 13.

4. Martin, *Local Studies Libraries*, p. 8.

5. Jill Barber (2002) 'Marketing', in Michael Dewe (ed.), *Local Studies Collection Management*. Aldershot: Ashgate, p. 143.

6. Barber, 'Marketing', p. 147.

8

Evaluation and appraisal

Introduction

This final chapter is concerned with the importance of ongoing evaluation and appraisal of electronic resources, focusing principally on local studies materials but, where appropriate, drawing in more general examples from the broader reference and enquiry sphere. The chapter is not concerned with the evaluation and appraisal of the local studies service per se but, more specifically, with the sources and, in particular, the digital dimension.

Evaluation and appraisal of information sources or services can generally be said to be undertaken for four main reasons: firstly, in order to ensure the reliability, accuracy and validity of the information provided to users; secondly, in order to save the time of the user by ensuring that he or she concentrates on the use of the most significant, current and authoritative information; thirdly, in order to provide a balanced view of the issues or arguments relating to a specific topic; and fourthly, in order to filter materials that may misinform either deliberately or accidentally. As the Internet has become a more commonplace tool in reference work it has become essential to look critically at the sources available through it and how they enhance the service provision:

While the Web is only one source of information and traditional sources will not, and should not, disappear, the Web is becoming a necessary source in reference service with its unique features. When it is used properly, Web sources can enhance reference service.[1]

In one of the first major studies carried out into the efficiency of the Internet as a tool for responding to reference questions, Zumalt and Pasiczynyuk (1998)[2] found that some 61.7 per cent of reference enquiries could be answered effectively and accurately using the Internet. They concluded that the Internet should figure prominently as a reference source and that it offered particularly significant potential for libraries with smaller amounts of reference stock.

The fact that the Internet offers no editorial or refereeing procedure has already been mentioned elsewhere in this book. Any individual or organisation can host a site and provide information but there is no guarantee that the material will be reliable, accurate or current. Consequently, scrutiny of sources and services is paramount. Smith, writing in 1997, identified two main aspects that need to be addressed:

(1) to decide whether an Internet information source should be linked to a resource guide or library web site, or (2) to judge the quality or appropriateness of information for a particular user or query.[3]

The reference library in general should act as a gateway and guide for users to reliable and authoritative sources of information on the Internet in order to maximise the exploitation of valuable resources and in order to save the time of both the user and staff in wading through the undifferentiated mass of material. This is, perhaps, also true for the local studies department but true in a different way. By its very nature, local studies is about specificity and, in many instances, the 'mass of material' simply does not exist. One of the fundamental challenges for local studies librarians is to decide whether the pre-eminence attached to the authority and currency of the source in other aspects of reference work really is directly transferable to the local studies context. The evidence would seem to suggest that it is not.

Evaluative criteria

Most traditional and long-established evaluative criteria are aimed specifically at printed reference or information sources, for example Katz's list of six evaluative criteria.[4] However, new criteria or interpretations of the traditional ones are being established for electronic sources. Katz's evaluative criteria can been viewed in this light:

- purpose – preface, documentation, online help facilities;
- authority, objectivity and fairness – little indication exists for many electronic sources (particularly Internet sources), and authors often remain unidentified;
- scope – the breadth and depth of coverage;
- audience or level;
- cost in various media;
- format – the arrangement, ease of retrieval, searchable fields.

There are a number of listings of criteria that may be used in evaluating Internet sites and these tend to be the focus of much recent literature on the evaluation of information. Many of these, however, focus on aesthetic or design aspects rather than on content and information utility.

Evaluation of digital information sources needs to be set within the context of user needs. Many of the criteria for evaluation of sources and services suggest a distinction between the professional and the lay researcher. Received wisdom on evaluation and appraisal would have it that the level of presentation may, for example, vary according to the understanding of the target audience. Professional researchers will need access to a comprehensive view of the significant, high-quality researched produced on a topic; a lay audience may only require a broad summary of the differing perspectives. Broadly speaking in reference and enquiry terms this may be the case. A huge gulf might indeed exist between one person's requirements for information on, say, chemical fertilisers and another's, one being the research scientist and the other being the gardener, one being highly educated the other being less so. However, this distinction (and with it many of the other evaluative criteria) might work in general reference terms but it is far less satisfactory within the context of local studies.

In order to understand why it is different for local studies it is necessary to go right back to the beginning, to a point made near the start of this book and to look at what the local studies collection is setting out to do. Essentially, it is necessary to understand how it defines itself. Chapter 1 of this book suggests three points which should be observed in terms of defining a local collection. It suggests that the topographical definition for coverage be transparent, that the aim in terms of comprehensive coverage be understood and that the format of material is irrelevant to the acquisition. It follows that if the first two points are carefully understood and observed then the third should follow naturally.

All three points also need to be observed in terms of the evaluation and appraisal of electronic sources but the topographic definition and comprehensive coverage within it are particularly significant. Limiting any collection's coverage by geography will inevitably have a profound impact on the range and type of materials available. Geographical limitations do not, however, make the traditional evaluative criteria redundant. It is still perfectly possible to consider sources and services (whether hard-copy or electronic) in terms of scope, reliability, currency, authority, accuracy and so on. However, seeking to have *comprehensive* coverage within that limited geographical area *does* change everything. No single information service (or indeed source) can ever be said to be truly comprehensive, even within particularly well-defined geographical limits. However, having comprehensiveness as an objective impacts greatly on the way in which we must treat evaluation and appraisal of local studies sources.

It is entirely likely that the 'good' local studies collection will strive for comprehensive coverage within its geographic limitations or parameters. This has long been applied to traditional printed formats. The good, the bad and the indifferent all have a place within the collection; the 'bad' item may be unreliable, inaccurate, lacking in authority but it may also contain one single paragraph that is priceless in local terms. Indeed, Old Parish Registers, often among the most heavily used sources in local studies, can also often be the most unreliable and most inaccurate. The scholarly multi-volume work on local flora and fauna by a nineteenth-century antiquarian and the 30-page paperback commemorating a local football team by a former player are, therefore, treated equally in the local studies collection not so much for their appeal to different levels or audiences but because they contribute equally to the notion of the collective memory of the community. By collecting such disparate items the collection manager is attempting to ensure comprehensive coverage. The goal of preserving the collective memory of the community is, in many respects, paramount.

This is not to say that evaluation and appraisal of sources within the local studies sphere must be crude and simplistic and lacking in refinement. What it does signify is that a much more pragmatic approach is required to evaluation of sources and services. It is perhaps necessary to look at an appropriate method of evaluating all local studies materials (regardless of format) in the first instance and then to attempt to understand how this may be applied to electronic sources and services at a community level.

An interesting parallel exists between electronic sources and local studies sources in general. It is often said that the Internet provides no editorial quality standards and no refereeing process and this is indeed the case looking at the Internet as a whole. However, many of the traditionally printed items that fill the shelves of local studies departments can be said to fall into exactly the same category. Countless small, local publications that, for example, chart the history of a village or a school or an organisation may well have been researched, compiled and written entirely by amateurs who have, in some way or another, found enough money to get the volume printed (as opposed to published). One of the strengths of local studies collections is the quantity of short publications that have been lovingly researched and produced by interested members of the community.

Having defined the scope of the collection itself and looked at what its objectives are, the next element which really needs to be addressed is the examination of evaluation and appraisal within the context of user needs. As the previous chapter points out, many local studies departments practised lifelong learning and social inclusion long before they became fashionable or trendy. Local studies departments are very familiar with self-improvers working on a particular piece of local research. Local studies departments and their staff have also proved themselves adept at reaching out into the community through their active liaison with local groups and organisations. In some ways, other parts of the library have been catching up in these respects in recent years.

The result of this is that local studies staff tend to have a good awareness of their user profile. Local studies tend to be a part of the library that people come back to time and time again, their researches are never completed and there always exists the potential for something new to come to light if they continue to look hard enough. This means that a significant proportion, perhaps even a majority, of users are keenly aware of how to examine and appraise the sources they are consulting even if many of them are without formal academic qualifications, having taught themselves to engage in local research to a professional degree. They may well be amateurs with no formal qualifications or with no idea of formal source criticism but through sheer determination they have come to grasp the limitations of sources and services and have developed skills in piecing together disparate materials.

Taken from the perspective of a local studies department, there is perhaps some degree of truth in accusations that librarians over-evaluate sources and services on behalf of users who are perfectly capable of making value judgements for themselves. This is not really a credible argument (and certainly not with regard to conventional reference and enquiry work). However, it is perhaps possible to say that local studies librarians have always exhibited a greater degree of trust in their users because the notion of comprehensiveness of coverage means that some degree of discrimination has to be adopted by users when looking at the materials and not simply because of the types of sources that are housed within the collection.

It is inescapable that local studies and local history investigations go hand-in-hand and a majority of users come into departments in order to carry out some sort of historical investigation whether that be for something that happened two months earlier or two hundred years earlier. Historical investigation depends on the sources that happen to have survived and this inevitably means that coverage is partial. While the stock acquisition policy might indeed strive for comprehensive coverage, it is obviously the case that it can only be comprehensive in terms of what actually exists. The result is that while it is laudable to seek to obtain everything on the area we become aware very quickly that the contemporary body of information, whether hard-copy or electronic, is based only on what has survived and that vital facts from the past are almost certainly going to be missing. This basic point teaches all who work in or use local studies departments a fundamental lesson – never put total faith in a single source.

No source – irrespective of its format – is absolutely reliable and totally accurate. No source is more authoritative than its author and no work can be more comprehensive than the sources it is drawn from. Within the local studies sphere, familiarity with the sources inevitably leads to scepticism; there is always the nagging suspicion that even the most reliable of sources can have got it wrong on occasions or has embellished a particular event or person in the past. This has an inevitable chain reaction beginning with a recognition of partial coverage and leading to an assumption of inaccuracy until proved otherwise until a fact can be corroborated using an alternative source. Multi-sourcing has always been central within local studies for that reason. The genealogist is particularly good at this, knowing that they should never accept something until they have seen the evidence, and preferably in two different places. One local studies librarian remarked:

> I'm always delighted when I hear a family historian, peering at an Old Parish Register on microfilm, say 'That just can't be right I must check that in…' and at that moment I know that they have 'got it' and they realise how all of these sources fit together.[5]

Evaluation and appraisal of local studies sources and services is not, therefore, the exclusive reserve of the librarian or the information professional. Many local studies users have developed these skills for themselves as the quote above indicates. If the collection does indeed aim for comprehensiveness within its geographical limits then users' evaluation skills are perhaps something to be strongly encouraged.

Given the fact that comprehensiveness is often seen as an essential objective of local studies collections it can come as no surprise that many local studies users also rank comprehensiveness very highly. In most cases, because the evidence is partial anyway, they would prefer to have as much material as it is humanly possible to gather before them. Local studies users prefer to make their own judgements based on the information in front of them and in the context of the particular subject that they are trying to investigate. In many instances in local studies, but particularly in genealogy, users will often be in a better position than the librarian to judge the reliability of a particular piece of information. Having studied their own family history extensively they will often be better placed to evaluate the credibility of a particular source as it relates to their own investigations. Many of these users will have taught themselves the skills and will have no formal or academic training in this source criticism.

However, there are, of course, issues associated with new users who are unfamiliar with the sources and their reliability. It can be argued, perhaps, that librarians introducing new users to the sources should comment on any problematic issues associated with them. Additionally, there may be issues for more experienced users where their lack of professional training might present problems. In particular, there may well be issues associated with materials in Latin or those which require palaeographic skills. However, these issues aside, it would be foolish to underestimate the levels of attainment achieved by 'lay' or 'amateur' researchers, and it would be equally foolish to underestimate their ability to view the sources and services as fallible.

Evaluating information sources

The evaluation and appraisal of electronic sources for local studies, regardless of whether they are delivered using CD-Rom or available online using the Internet, must fall into two distinct categories. It is fair to say that no one-size-fits-all approach can be adopted for electronic sources within the local sphere. The first of the distinct categories is the 'global' sources that also provide a local dimension. So, in terms of global sources such as Family Search, GenForum or Censuses online, it is perfectly possible for the librarian to use the conventional evaluative criteria that have been laid down by various authors (Katz, Large, Basch, Wilkinson, Harris, Smith and so on) in the field. The second category is that of local materials online, those which go so far to contribute to the idea of comprehensiveness, and for which a much more pragmatic and, indeed, relaxed approach needs to be taken.

In the first instance, it is perhaps important to look at some of the evaluative criteria that have been suggested by authors in this sphere and see how they relate to the global information sources that have a part to play in local studies service provision. Many of these evaluative criteria seem more suited to appraising sources such as online indexing or abstracting services but they can equally be applied to many of the global electronic sources used in local studies (such as genealogical or biographical databases).

There are a large number of criteria that may be considered in evaluating Internet sites. These may be prioritised in different ways depending upon the use that is to be made of the site and the particular information need that is being served. On occasion the criteria may be in conflict: for example, it may not be possible for a site to be both very current and highly accurate, or a site may be valued because it gives access to a wide range of opinions on a subject rather than to a very select assembly of highly authoritative views. Equally, criteria may be mutually difficult to satisfy, for example seeking to be both highly current and accurate, when error checking and refereeing processes are likely to slow the process down.

A number of writers have attempted to create evaluative criteria for the digital environment from modifications of W.A. Katz's basic evaluative criteria; others have created to entirely new sets such as those by Basch (1996), Wilkinson, Bennett and Oliver (1997), Smith (1997) and Harris (1997).

These evaluative criteria are undeniably very useful in a general reference context. Wilkinson, Bennett and Oliver (1997) suggest eleven evaluative criteria and quality indicators for electronic sources:

1. Site access and usability

2. Resource identification and documentation

3. Author identification

4. Authority of author

5. Information structure and design

6. Relevance and scope of content

7. Validity of content

8. Accuracy and balance of content

9. Navigation within the document

10. Quality of links

11. Aesthetic and affective aspects

Smith (1997) suggests eight evaluative criteria for Internet information sources:

1. Scope – covering the breadth, depth, time period, format of resources included.

2. Content – fact or opinion, originality, utility, reliability of links, accuracy, authority, currency, uniqueness, quality of writing.

3. Graphics and multimedia design – visual effects, audio and video support, virtual reality modelling.

4. Purpose and audience – clearly stated, does it fulfil purpose? level, does it satisfy needs of intended audience?

5. Reviews – in journals, gateways.

6. Workability – user friendliness, good help support, effective menu design and readability of screens.

7. Searching – information retrieval capacity, is the search engine intuitive? does it rank results? is the whole resource indexed? is the organisation of the site logical? appropriate arrangement of materials, interactive features, good connectivity.

8. Cost – telecommunications, connection charges, subscriptions, site licences.

These criteria are useful listings but few sources will satisfy the demands of all of these criteria simultaneously. However, a systematic appraisal can only be developed based upon a consideration of each. In most cases, these evaluative recommendations are much more applicable to the type of information sources and services found in reference departments generally. It would certainly be possible to apply them to sources such as International Pharmaceutical Abstracts, ERIC or the Trade and Industry database. From this perspective, it is obvious therefore that they can also be quite easily applied to evaluate and appraise sources such as Family Search or the various electronic sources covering censuses and biographical databases, all of which might feature in the electronic arsenal of a local studies collection.

What these evaluative criteria are not suited to are the mass of 'ordinary' local sites that have proliferated on the Internet. These criteria are not well suited to dealing with the website of a local football club or a church, of an individual family history or a site that has a collection of old photographs of a particular town. While it is undeniably the case that some local sites have been created and developed to the highest possible professional standards, many have been created by well-meaning amateurs who have no particular background in either information design or website creation.

A simple example will demonstrate the difficulties with such evaluative criteria for truly local sites. A congregation member with an interest in the Internet has designed and now hosts a website for a local church. The site might be perfectly respectable but makes no reference to the other local churches in the town, to the synagogue down the street or to the mosque on the other side of town. The site does, however, include a religious message from the minister. Clearly the site can be deemed to be entirely biased and contains no balance whatsoever. The creator is nothing more than an interested amateur and the site has poor navigational techniques, no searching facility, a couple of dead links and multimedia devices are non-existent. So on aesthetic and information design criteria it fails again. The section dealing with the history of the church has been well-researched but has a number of typing errors and two or three glaring factual mistakes. It is not clear who has written the text and some of the material is not referenced. So, in accuracy terms, it fails for a third time. However, the website contains six photographs which show the rebuilding of the church in the nineteenth century and one shows the building that was on the site previously. The local studies collection does not hold copies of these. This, in itself, is enough to make an otherwise uninspiring and perhaps even inaccurate site of huge importance.

Thus a local site can fail on virtually all of the recognised evaluative criteria for Internet information sources but because of the inclusion of something unique which aids the concept of the comprehensive memory of the community we must be prepared to abandon these criteria and endorse the site, warts and all. Carrying out such an evaluation of a local site will highlight the failings but, as with the example above, it will also highlight what is very important. Such an evaluation may lead the local studies librarian to attempt to gain copies of the unique images for deposit in the collection itself.

No study comparable to that of Zumalt and Pasiczynyuk (1998) has been undertaken for local studies but it is certain that the percentage of enquiries capable of being answered using the Internet would be much smaller (and if genealogical questions that utilise Family Search were removed the figure would be even less). Indeed considerable scope exists for a study to look specifically at the use (or otherwise) of the Internet in responding to local studies enquiries. Generally, local studies, by its very nature, will always rely more heavily on the traditionally published materials. However, increasingly electronic reference sources (largely but not exclusively CD-Rom ones) are making an impact. Ultimately, in local studies collections the hard copy and the digital will, almost certainly, coexist for ever. The crucial dynamic of local studies – that partial (hard-copy) sources complement each other – has always existed and is widely recognised. In the future more partial sources may be added; this time, however, they may be digital ones. A local studies collection is and always has been the sum of its parts and this is likely to continue.

Evaluating local sources

The following are not necessarily indicators which should be used in the stock selection or acquisition process but rather are factors which can be used to assess the value and positioning of sources:

- Localness
- Originality
- Contribution
- Authority
- Level
- Integrity
- Timescale
- Interaction
- Effectiveness
- Support

Localness

If a local studies collection has as its principal objective comprehensive coverage of the local area then the most important evaluative criteria must relate to that sense of locality. In essence, this relates back to the question posed at the beginning of this book about how local is local and how do collection managers define the scope and parameters of the locality in terms of the coverage of the collection. The local value of some sources (either hardcopy or electronic) may very well be partial. This is particularly noticeable with works about particular subjects or themes. For example, a work on steam railways or women's emancipation may not be easily identifiable in local terms on first inspection but may well contain references that have an obvious community relevance. Local content may sometimes legitimately be sacrificed if other aspects are significant. For example, it might well be the case that the inherent interest in a work lies in the fact that the author or creator is local rather than the subject matter.

Originality

This can be looked at from a variety of different perspectives. It may be that a source genuinely does have something new to say. It may be the first time that disparate sources have been pulled together to create a focused investigation into a particular place, person or subject. In this case, the originality is obvious and apparent. However, originality is also closely tied to the question of uniqueness which is widely recognised as being one of the key features of local studies collections. A source, be it hard-copy or electronic, may very well fail on a variety of evaluative criteria but is deemed to be essential and core because it does, in some way, contain unique materials not found elsewhere. The example provided earlier of the well-meaning amateur who has created a website for a local church and who has, in the course of their investigations, unearthed six pictures of the building of the church 120 years ago demonstrates this. The remainder of the material might be of poor quality (in the eyes of information professionals) or it may indeed replicate information widely held elsewhere but the inclusion of those six unique photographs renders it invaluable and highlights its originality.

Contribution

The contribution that the source makes to the collection should be considered. It might very well be assumed that 'c' should stand for comprehensiveness since much has been made of this as the fundamental precept of local studies. However, comprehensiveness within local studies is derived from the sum of the various parts of the collection, not necessarily from the sources individually. Individual local studies sources are seldom comprehensive (in the sense that information professionals tend to mean) because the evidence on which many are based is inevitably partial and because ultimately comprehensiveness is difficult to measure in a very local context. However, these individual sources should be examined in terms of the contribution that they make to the comprehensiveness of the collection as whole. It may well be that a source is far from comprehensive in its coverage of a particular subject; it may well be that it, like the local studies collection itself, has a particular geographical bias or a time-period bias. However, viewed in the light of the coverage of this particular subject in the collection as a whole, the work might make a valuable contribution. Viewed in the light of the other eight or ten sources on that subject this new addition, however slight or partial its individual content might be, may well be the one to ensure that the collection as a whole attains near comprehensiveness on that particular subject. For example, a history of railway developments in western England might only contain a handful of paragraphs that are of true local worth but that worth might be inestimable

Authority

This is perhaps the most difficult area to assess in terms of local studies collections. It can be argued that authority is inevitably sacrificed if the principal objective of the collection is comprehensiveness. However, the individual source itself can, of course, still be examined in terms of its own authority and reliability. Authority can be more difficult to assess in the digital world because very often websites provide little or no indication of who the creator or author is and, equally significantly, provide little or no indication of where the information came from and whether the conclusions being drawn are legitimate, objective and based on sound research techniques. In some cases, the partial evidence which exists in terms of historical evidence is overlooked in favour of sweeping generalisations, vague comments and unsubstantiated conclusions. It is particularly important for the librarian to be aware of this in the electronic sphere where there is no editorial gate-keeping to prevent inaccurate material being disseminated.

The natural temptation for the librarian is simply to ignore the existence of sites which do not conform to the traditional rules governing authority, validity, reliability and accuracy.

Sometimes there is a perfectly understandable desire to ignore sites that might be regarded as 'suspect'. However, this risks alienating local groups (and potentially, therefore, users of the collection) and also runs the risk of ignoring some potentially useful information. It is better for the local studies librarian to acknowledge these sites – thus adhering to the concept of contribution to comprehensiveness – but to warn users that they are not responsible for the content or accuracy of external sites. This should be done for *all* external sites whether their quality and authority is in question or not. The attachment of a simple warning message to hyperlinks on a local studies gateway stating that 'You are now leaving Littletown Library's website. We are not responsible for the accuracy of the content of external sites' should suffice.

Level

The level of the material included on any site is particularly important, more so since most libraries want to be seen as being as inclusive as possible. For local studies departments this is often a particular challenge as many of the sources were not created with contemporary notions of accessibility in mind. Equally, sources created for one purpose are now often used for another; Old Parish Registers are a particularly good example. They were created essentially as part of religious administration yet are now principally used for genealogy. Images are particularly useful in this regard and their role should not be underestimated. Whereas a text may indeed have a natural level (being appropriate for postgraduate students but not for children) a photograph can be understood on a variety of different levels by a much wider audience, indeed by almost everyone. Consequently, it is important to attempt to address the issues associated with the level of material, for these influence and affect the accessibility of information and ultimately the inclusiveness of the collection. As has been mentioned in earlier chapters, it may be necessary to produce guides to particular sources (and these are ripe for uploading onto the Internet) in order to explain what the material is about and how to make sense of it.

Integrity

Electronic sources require to be viewed carefully and analysed in a vigilant fashion. This is perhaps most obviously the case with those tools that are basically electronic reference sources (and there are many in the field of e-genealogy in particular). The overall integrity of these sources require to be evaluated in terms of the many standard techniques and criteria that are available for the appraisal of electronic sources. However, in terms of websites, often created by individuals or small groups, slightly more flexibility should be used. The local studies librarian has always been confronted with the paradox of providing high-quality information while also seeking to acquire, preserve and disseminate the complete record of the community and its people. In many respects, these decisions are best left to the professionals on the ground who understand the sources and understand the locality and who are in the best position to make value judgements. In reality, electronic sources and hard copy, often archival, will continue to coexist, and probably always will. And, in many cases, their integrity will be best assessed in terms of the contribution (and it may be a very partial contribution) that they make to the collection as a whole and how they complement the multitude of other sources available.

Time period

Many studies have sought to explore the significance of the various criteria for users. Often currency is highly significant. The need for currency in relation to financial or corporate information tends to be paramount and obviously so. It is often highly important for researchers to have access to very recent developments but this will be measured in their case by a desire to ensure access to the most significant and valid research, which is often published in scholarly journals which tend to have a slow turn-around in terms of publication. However, local studies has always been different; it often positively seeks out old, out-of-date materials and then positively seeks to maintain these indefinitely, often in perpetuity. It is important, in the digital environment, that all time-periods are represented to some degree, thus demonstrating the extent of the collection itself. Currency in website terms is, however, important and from a purely practical in-house perspective regular maintenance and updating is of paramount importance. Websites that have not been updated recently turn off visitors who tend to think that organisations which cannot be bothered to do anything to the site will not be particular helpful or receptive.

Interaction

It is important not to look at sources in isolation but within the context of the established parts of the collection. Replication of coverage within local studies is not necessarily a bad thing and, to a certain extent, this will always happen because new sources of information tend to draw heavily on the existing ones within a local studies context. Scrutiny of new sources should seek to identify what evidence there is of interaction with other primary and secondary sources that the collection may already possess or, at least, have access to. The cyclical nature of local history is demonstrated by the fact that many local history websites will have been created drawing heavily on the material maintained by local studies departments in the first place. In its own way this is a means of examining content and assessing the authority of the source. Additionally, however, it may well also be a means of assessing how complementary the source is.

Effectiveness

The creation of a local studies website is an ongoing process. Alas, a number of collections seem to be content, once they have uploaded a few brief pages, with providing a description of the contents of the physical collection itself. Little further effort is made to exploit the resources that actually lie within the collection. This is not an effective approach. Other collections have uploaded material for which there is little demand and which holds little appeal to users. Content selection is vital. If time and effort are to be expended on digital solutions then finding *appropriate* materials that are *effective* in terms of meeting the aims and objectives of the organisation and the collection must be crucial. Users, both local and remote, will soon tire of such a narrow and disappointing effort. Given the widespread access to electronic sources they will go elsewhere and potentially miss out on the unique material that the collection will, undoubtedly, possess. Monitoring and evaluation of the site must be an ongoing process to chart the effectiveness of the site both to the organisation and to users. Online user questionnaires should be developed and implemented on at least an annual basis. Guest-books and e-mails should be scrutinised to see what is working and what is not.

Support

A website is not simply a passive tool. As has been mentioned earlier in this book, it is a living and growing mechanism. While it is desirable to include interactive elements in a website it is vital, perhaps pre-eminently so, to include support – both technical help about the site itself and practical assistance about the mechanics of using the sources and undertaking local studies investigations. Providing support is something that all librarians are very good at and this is something which is a necessity in cyberspace.

Application in cyberspace

Virtual communities and virtual local studies are about social inclusion. They are about serving communities that have found a renewed enthusiasm for their roots. Globally, the sense of *heimat* has re-emerged as a potent force. The Internet and the creation of digital records about people, places, events and subjects enable many users to feel that they are overcoming the diaspora that perhaps took their parents or grandparents away from a particular community.

Local studies departments face many challenges in the coming decade. Principal among these is their relationship with the Internet. By definition, local studies *are* specific and partial (and this is what that separates them from other parts of the library service). The entire approach to managing local studies is distinct from the rest of the library and equally the approach to digital technology (evaluation and appraisal included) must be set apart from the rest of the reference and enquiry sector.

As has been outlined earlier in this chapter, there are many different criteria that can be applied to evaluation and appraisal, both for the conventional sources and for the electronic. The Maori culture in New Zealand relied heavily on the use of oral history. In selecting potential candidates to be oral historians, the Maoris laid down five principal criteria[6] which had to be met:

- Receive the information with accuracy.
- Store the information with integrity beyond doubt.

- Retrieve the information without amendments.

- Apply appropriate judgements in the use of the information.

- Pass on the information appropriately.

Perhaps this is as good a set of evaluative criteria for digital local studies as anything.

The Internet serves two distinct but interrelated purposes within the context of a local studies department. Firstly, it is about widening access to new users (both locally within the community and further afield). It is about the notions of social inclusion and lifelong learning (much mentioned within this book). It is about maximising the potential of the collection and moving it forward in new and challenging and dynamic ways. Secondly, however, it is also about capturing, securing and preserving the wealth of data and information that is increasingly becoming available *only* in digital form. As has been mentioned earlier, the Internet is being used by individuals and organisations to publish their own researches and promote their own activities. In the past, local studies collections would have sought to collect this sort of material in hard copy in a systematic and organised fashion. The Internet has necessitated a change in this. Identifying and retrieving Internet sources on the local community must become a central objective of the local studies department. It may even be that the library needs to seek more innovative solutions in order to achieve this goal. Burning local sites (which may be transitory or ephemeral) onto CD-Rom may be one solution. Another may be attempting to create a local electronic deposit mechanism. If local studies departments do not grasp this nettle then future generations may find that there is a significant gap in the research materials available to them. This would be the supreme paradox given the otherwise immense benefits of the digital age.

Notes

1. Su Di (1999) 'Sources in reference service', *Reference Librarian*, 65: 161–76.
2. J.R. Zumalt and R.W. Pasiczynyuk (1998) 'The Internet and reference services', *Reference and User Services Quarterly*, 38(2): 165–72.
3. A.G. Smith (1997) 'Testing the surf: criteria for evaluating Internet information resources', *Public Access Computer Systems Review*, 8(3).
4. W.A. Katz (1997) *Introduction to Reference Work*, 7th edn. London: McGraw-Hill.
5. Private source (a local studies librarian).
6. I am grateful to Professor Derek Law of Strathclyde University for drawing my attention to these.

Bibliography

This bibliography contains references to those items consulted for this work. For a full bibliography of Local Studies see Diana Dixon's *Local Studies Librarianship: A World Bibliography* (London: Library Association, 2001).

Basch, R. (1996) *Secrets of the Super Net Searchers: The Reflections, Revelations, and Hard-won Wisdom of 35 of the World's Top Internet Searchers*. Wilton, CT: Pemberton Press.

Cochrane, C. (1985) 'Public libraries and the changing nature of oral history', *Audiovisual Librarian*, 11(4): 201–7.

Dewe, M. (ed.) (1987) *Local Studies Collections: A Manual*, Vol. 1. Aldershot: Gower.

Dewe, M. (ed.) (1991) *Local Studies Collections: A Manual*, Vol. 2. Aldershot: Gower.

Dewe, M. (ed.) (2002) *Local Studies Collection Management*. Aldershot: Ashgate.

Di, Su (1999) 'Sources in reference services', *Reference Librarian*, 65: 161–76.

Dixon, D. (2001) *Local Studies Librarianship: A World Bibliography*. London: Library Association.

Ermoin, C. (1999) 'An investigation into the use of local studies sections and archives and their links with the user's sense of local identity: a comparison between the north-east of Scotland and Manche in Low Normandy'. MSc thesis, Robert Gordon University, Aberdeen.

Falk, H. (1999) 'View through the display window', *Electronic Library*, 17(4): 263–7.

FitzHugh, T. (1998) *Dictionary of Genealogy*, 5th edn. London: A & C Black.

Friggens, G. (1998) 'Local studies centres', *Local Studies Librarian*, 17(2): 8–11.

Glogoff, L.G and Glogoff, S. (1998) 'Using the World Wide Web for community outreach: enriching library services to the community', *Internet Reference Services Quarterly*, 3(1): 15–26.

Hampson, A. (1998) 'Managing a digitisation project', *Managing Information*, 5(10): 25–32.

Harris, O. (1997) 'United we stand – Croydon's multi-disciplinary historical database', *ITs News*, 33: 17–21.

Harris, R., Feather, J. and Evans, M. (2000) *The Legal Deposit of Local Publications: A Case Study of Leicestershire, Leicester and Rutland*. London: Library and Information Commission.

Hayes, M. (1997) 'Sleeping with the enemy', *Local Studies Librarian*, 16(1): 2–5.

Hobbs, J.L. (1973) *Local History and the Library*, ed. George A. Carter. London: André Deutsch.

Hume, E. (2003) Results of local studies cataloguing questionnaire. Available at *http://www.oakedge.demon.co.uk* (May).

Jukvam, D., Skråmm, W.H. and Våge, N.S. (1990) 'Local history stored on computer: the Fet project', *Scandinavian Public Library Quarterly*, 23(3): 23–7.

Katz, W.A. (1997) *Introduction to Reference Work*, 7th edn. London: McGraw-Hill.

Lewis, M.J. and Lloyd-Jones, R. (1996) *Using Computers in History: A Practical Guide*. London: Routledge.

Library of Congress (2003) *Local History and Genealogy Reading Room*. Available at *http://www.loc.gov/rr/ genealogy* (accessed 2003).

Local History News (various).

Local History Magazine (various).

Marchant, P. and Hume, E. (1998) 'Visiting Knowsley's past', *Library Association Record*, 100(9): 468–9.

Martin, D. (2002) *Local Studies Libraries*, 2nd edn. London: Library Association.

Maxted, I. (1997) 'What's new? What's cool? Surf Devon and see', *Local Studies Librarian*, 16(1): 10–11.

Matkin, C. and Gordon, R.A. (2000) 'Consulting the customer: a survey of local studies library users in Derbyshire', *Local Studies Librarian*, 19(1): 2–5.

Neilson, K. and Willett, P. (1999) 'United Kingdom regional newspapers on the World Wide Web', *Aslib Proceedings*, 50(9): 78–90.

New Library: The People's Network (1997) Library and Information Commission for the Department of Culture, Media and Sport. Available at *http://www.ukoln.ac.uk/ services/lic/newlibrary/full.html* (accessed 2003).

Paul, D. (1995) 'Training 2000? Local and family history in libraries', *Librarian Career Development*, 3(4): 4–9.

People's Network (2003) Available at *http://www .peoplesnetwork.gov.uk/* (accessed May).

Petty, M. (1996) 'Networking local studies', *Local Studies Librarian*, 15(1): 2–5.

Phillips, F. (1995) *Local History Collections in Libraries*. Englewood, CO: Libraries Unlimited.

Rudyard, N. (2001) 'Old wine in new bottles: local history in the digital age', *Local Studies Librarian*, 20(1): 2.

Sherwood, L.E. (1998) 'Discovering the buffalo story robes: a case for cross domain information strategies', *Computers and the Humanities*, 32: 57–64.

Smith, A.G. (1997) 'Testing the surf: criteria for evaluating Internet information resources', *Public Access Computer Systems Review*, 8(3); available at *http://info.lib.uh.edu/pr/v8/n3/smit8n3.html*.

Usherwood, B. and Linley, R. (2000) 'Evaluating equity in public library services', *Journal of Librarianship and Information Science*, 32(2): 72–81.

Williams, P. and Nicholas, D. (1998) 'The Internet, a regional newspaper and the provision of "valued-added" information', *Aslib Proceedings*, 43(2): 255–63.

Wilkinson, G.L., Bennett, L. and Oliver, K. (1997) 'Evaluating criteria and indicators of quality for Internet resources', *Educational Technology*, 37(3): 52–9.

Wilson, S. (1998) 'Knowsley local history, using the Internet to enhance access', *Journal of the Society of Archivists*, 19(2): 199–209.

Winterbotham, D. and Crosby, A. (1998) *The Local Studies Library: A Handbook for Local Historians*. Salisbury: British Association for Local History.

Zumalt, J.R. and Pasiczynyuk, R.W. (1998) 'The Internet and reference services', *Reference and User Services Quarterly*, 38(2): 165–72.

Index